W9-BYH-317

Loving God
with All
Your Mind

Elizabeth George

HARVEST HOUSE PUBLISHERS
Eugene, Oregon 97402

Cover by DesignTeam, Grand Rapids, Michigan

Cover illustration by Sandy Lynam Clough

LOVING GOD WITH ALL YOUR MIND

Copyright © 1994 by Harvest House Publishers
Eugene, Oregon 97402

Library of Congress-in-Publication Data

George, Elizabeth, 1944–
    Loving God with all your mind / Elizabeth George.
      p. cm.
    ISBN 1-56507-861-6
    1. Christian women—Religious life. 2. Christian life—1960–
I. Title.
BV4527.G46 1994
248.8'43—dc20

93-33928
CIP

Printed in the United States of America.

02 03 04 05 06 07 08 09 / BC / 20 19 18 17 16

To, for, and because of Jim

Contents

— ❧ —

Invitation to a Changed Life

———— 🙶 ————

This book began with a phone call from the coordinator of the women's Bible study at our church. When she invited me to teach a class, she told me that I could teach anything I wanted to.

Excited about teaching but not sure what topic to focus on, I began to pray, "God, what message would be most helpful for these women? What could I say that would most enable You to work in their lives?" I also began to think about what messages from God's Word had been most helpful for me and where God had done His greatest work in my life.

The answer to my prayers came one morning as I was reviewing some of the passages from Scripture which I've memorized through the years. Thinking about a particular verse, I realized, "The truth of this Scripture has changed my life. Why don't I share this with the women? After all, if it helped me, why couldn't it help others?" I made a note of that verse.

Over the next several days, I gathered six powerful passages that I knew God could use in these women's lives, and these six verses are the basis of this book. Each verse carries with it many memories because each one has played—and continues to play—a key role in my spiritual growth. God uses these Scriptures to give me hope and help me overcome negative emotions, damaging thoughts, and destructive attitudes. God has used them to transform my thinking and give me a higher standard for my behavior as His child.

7

Having selected these six passages, I then began to pray a different prayer—"God, help me show these women how You can use Your Word to change their lives by transforming their thoughts! Help me to show women how to love You with all their mind—and continue to teach me!"

Experiencing God's Love

In Matthew 22, an expert in the law asks Jesus which is the greatest commandment of all. Jesus answers, "You shall love the Lord your God with all your heart and with all your soul, and with all your mind" (verse 37). Knowing Jesus' command is one thing; doing it is another. Exactly how are we to obey Jesus' command? What does it mean for you and me to love God with all our mind? That is what this book is all about.

Key to loving God with all our mind is truly experiencing His love for us. On our own power, we cannot change the way we think, but when we draw near to God and spend time getting to know Him by getting to know His Word, He uses the truths there to transform how we think. When we feel weak or overwhelmed by life, He can use Scriptures to give us strength. He can use the truths we find in His Word to fortify us to go on.

I like to think of God's Holy Word as an instrument He can use in our life to guide, comfort, correct, rebuke, and teach. The passages we commit to memory are like a surgeon's sterilized tools carefully arranged on instrument trays and ready for His expert use. When there is a need in our life, God can pick up exactly the verse we need and cut right to our heart. He has done so for me, and I know He will do so for you.

Also key to loving God with all our mind are the choices you and I make. We can choose to dwell on the negative, on our weakness, and on our pain, or we can let those things turn us to God. Regardless of how life looks or feels, we can make the deliberate decision to yield to God's wisdom and His ways. We can choose, for instance, to:

- Work on what is real rather than worry about what is unreal.
- Reach forward and press on rather than remaining a prisoner of the past.
- Believe the truths of the Bible rather than trust our emotions.
- Act on what is revealed in Scripture rather than on what appears to be.

By making these choices, we are choosing to love God with all our mind. The result is what I call "spiritual mental health," that peace and well-being which the Spirit gives when we think and act on the truths of the Bible.

The Power of God's Word

Even though this principle and these six Scriptures had made a significant difference in my thought life, I was not prepared for the women's response to the class. These women were excited about God's Word and its power in their lives. Their desire to learn more led to a second and third semester and the study of additional verses. Soon, women from other churches (some even outside the state) wanted me to share these principles and these Scriptures with them.

Also, as women wrote to me asking for tapes and a workbook, they shared testimonies of victory and change in their lives. They were experiencing the power of God and His Word. Their lives were changing as they began to think and act scripturally. Finally, it was suggested that perhaps a broader audience could benefit if these truths were put in writing. And, as I write this book, that is my prayer.

The scriptural principles presented in this book are both universal and effective because they represent a biblical way of thinking and acting. Know that God will greatly use these principles and these six passages from Scripture in your life as you live out your faith in Christ. He will use them to draw you closer to Him and to release His power in your life.

Although you may be quite familiar with some, if not all, of the six passages I've chosen, I invite you to join me in discovering anew the life-giving and transforming power of these biblical truths. After all, looking at life's challenges from God's perspective and relying on Him to help you face them will indeed change your life. As you open yourself to God's presence and see Him use Scripture to guide and change your thoughts, you will find yourself, in obedience to Christ, loving God with all your mind.

Elizabeth George

1

Thinking on God's Truth

——————— ❧ ———————

*Whatsoever things are true...
think on these things.*
Philippians 4:8 (KJV)

——————— ❧ ———————

Because my husband, Jim, is in the ministry, our phone rings a lot, and that morning many years ago was no different. As I hurried across the family room to answer another call, I prayed my standard on-the-way-to-the-phone prayer—"God, whoever it is, whatever it is, help me."

That prayer, however, did not prepare me for the startling request this caller made. The woman, a member of our church, explained that she had met with one of the pastors that morning because of her tendency toward depression. At the end of the counseling session, he had given her some homework. The assignment was "Call Liz George and ask her how she overcame her struggle with depression."

Too shocked to respond, all I could do was ask for some time to think about my answer. As I hung up the phone, a tidal wave of emotions washed over me. One was concern for this woman. So few people—and, sadly, so few Christian women—face their problems to the point of seeking advice. Even fewer do what the counselor advises. Here was a woman asking for help—and asking for help from me.

I felt real empathy for my new friend, but I also felt betrayed. I didn't like hearing that a pastor had talked about me. Although the fact that he and Jim served together made us part of the staff family, never had any of us discussed my difficulties with depression. I wasn't pleased to be characterized as a woman who battled with depression, even though it was true. Besides, I thought I'd kept up a strong, capable front, but obviously this pastor had noticed.

I was also feeling pain. As you read this book, you will discover that one key to loving God with all our mind is not dwelling on the past or on unpleasant memories. Yet to help this woman, I would need to once again look closely at the painful past. As I made myself remember those darker days, I recalled my morning routine. . . .

I would stand at the kitchen sink, looking out the window, thinking long and hard until my thoughts pulled me down so far that tears began streaming down my cheeks into the dishwater. After the dishes came the housework. As I went from room to room, I felt oppressed and numb. A heavy, dark fog had settled in my head. Even in the sunshine of midday, I wanted to close my eyes. With my eyes shut, the fog would go away. Everything would be black, and I wouldn't have to keep groping my way along. . . .

How had my life changed since those days? What had helped me get past those dark and heavy moods? What had freed me from that almost-immobilizing depression? Was there some key I could pass on, some hope and help I could offer? This woman needed to know.

"Think on These Things"

As I mentally journeyed back to those unhappy years, I saw how God had worked in my life through three specific practices. The first was memorizing Scripture. Having been told—like every Christian—that I should memorize Scripture and not knowing that I had an option, I had dutifully begun to memorize passages from God's Word. I wrote Bible verses on index cards which I carried with me, taped on mirrors, laid on the breakfast table, and placed on the windowsill over my kitchen sink. I was doing what I knew was right, but I was quite unaware of the great benefits I would reap.

The second habit I was cultivating was meditating on Scripture. I had learned a method for meditating on God's Word in Carole Mayhall's book *From the Heart of a Woman.*[1] Reading Jim Downing's book *Meditation: The Bible Tells You How*[2] had also helped. Furthermore, the Moody Bible Institute's Scripture memory course I had enrolled in required meditation exercises for the assigned Scriptures.[3] Again, I knew that I was doing what was right, but I didn't know how helpful meditating on Scripture would actually prove to be.

The third and most challenging practice I was trying to master was obedience. It wasn't always easy to do what God was telling me to do in the verses I was memorizing and meditating on. But I knew that God had given us His Word to show us how to live and that I needed to *do* what it says, not just *know* what it says (Matthew 7:21). Again, little did I know at the time how God would use these three practices to remove the bars of depression that held me prisoner.

One morning as I was standing at the sink washing dishes, I was looking at the index card that was propped up on the windowsill. The memory verse was Philippians 4:8, a long verse which had been hard for me to learn. As I reviewed the verse, I counted the eight virtues of a Christian's thought life on my fingers to make sure I didn't leave one out.

Because I had meditated on Philippians 4:8 as a whole, I already knew it was a guideline for the kinds of thoughts which God would have occupy my mind. But I had never thought about each component separately. That morning I decided to take the verse apart while I washed the dishes.

Going through a routine exercise designed for unpacking the meaning of Scripture, I said out loud, "Finally, brethren, whatsoever things are true" and asked, "What does 'true' mean?" Obviously it means truth, the truth of Scripture, and the truth as opposed to lies. But true also means real: What is true is what is real. The door of understanding cracked open for me.

Continuing with the exercise, I then asked, "Is there a command to obey?" I pondered the words "think on these things." Stated in the positive, God is issuing the command, "Let your mind dwell on what is true or real." Turning the words around to the negative, the same command would be "Do not think on things that are not true or real."

This realization was my breakthrough. The darkness of my depression began to lift as the light of God's Word flooded into my mind. Here, in Philippians 4:8, God was telling me not to think about anything that wasn't true or real, and I needed to put this truth into practice. It has been estimated, however, that ten thousand thoughts pass through the human mind in one day. Obeying God's command would not be easy, but I also knew that God is at work to help us accomplish whatever He asks us to do.

Excited about my discovery, I started to evaluate my daily thoughts in light of the first few words of Philippians 4:8. Was I thinking about what was true or real? Over the next few weeks as I asked this question of the ideas in my mind, I began to realize that God had a solution for my long struggle with depression and that His Word offered hope for my moodiness. That solution and that hope lay in keeping my thoughts within the biblical boundaries of Philippians 4:8 (KJV)—"What-soever things are true [or real] . . . think on these things." These few words helped me take a significant first step toward spiritual mental health, and this Scripture continues to correct my unhealthy thinking. When we hold our thoughts up against God's standards of what is true and what is real, we can recognize and, with His help, learn to release many of our negative emotions, damaging thoughts, and destructive attitudes.

Healthy and Godly Thinking

A healthy thought life—a thought life that is pleasing to God—comes out of a close relationship with Him. After all, the God who loves us is at work within us to make us the women He would have us be, women who love Him with our mind as well as our heart. Through His Word, God calls us to use our mind to think about what is true and real. Once we determine what is true and real, we can then function according to these facts instead of our feelings or fantasies.

When we aren't functioning according to what is real, it is much like trying to function when you have a fever or the flu. You know how limited you are when you're not healthy. Even though you continue to fulfill your responsibilities, something is missing. The demands of each task and your body's ability to respond are out of synch. You may do your work, but there is little, if any, enthusiasm. Many times tasks are half done or done poorly. Poor physical health means less energy and lesser performance.

The same thing happens in the spiritual realm. Like a virus, our thoughts have the ability to drain our energy and cripple our usefulness. Our thoughts can, however, also be a source of strength when we dwell on the powerful truths of Scripture and let God work through those truths to change our way of thinking. Women who know God's Word and focus on those thoughts, which are based in reality, will be energized by such healthy thinking. So what do thoughts based in reality look like? The Bible provides guidelines for healthy thinking about God, ourselves, and relationships and, as we'll see in the next chapter, about the past, the future, and the challenges of the present.

Thinking About God

If we are to love God with all our mind, we need to be sure our ideas about God are accurate, biblical, and true. Inaccurate and unbiblical thoughts about God can block His power in our life. Another crucial step toward loving God with all our mind is determining to place the Bible's truths above everything we think or feel. We must guard against allowing our thoughts or feelings to override the great truths of Scripture.

First John 1:9, for instance, sets forth the important truth that, "if we confess our sins, He is faithful and righteous to forgive us our sins and to cleanse us from all unrighteousness." Although this statement guarantees that God forgives our sins, I have been guilty of saying, after a time of confession, "But I don't *feel* forgiven." When I do this, I am allowing my feelings to take precedence over the rock-solid doctrinal truth of the forgiveness of sins available to us through Christ. On other occasions I say, "But I don't think God could really forgive me. ˙ Again, I'm allowing my thoughts to take precedence over the Word of God. You and I are forgiven, regardless of our feelings and thoughts. To think we are not forgiven is to think a lie. When my feelings and thoughts are running counter to what Scripture teaches, I need to stop and ask, "But, Liz, what is true?" The answer is always the same: The Bible is true, not my feelings or thoughts. Having reminded myself of that, I then choose to "think forgiven."

After I shared this personal example at a Christian women's conference, one woman wrote, "For a long time now, my thoughts have been, 'But I don't feel forgiven' or 'Was I really saved to begin with?' I have confessed my sin over and over, and I hassle with it constantly. Reviewing this principle and going over this Scripture is already beginning to correct my thinking."

Our thoughts and feelings can have us doubting God's love for us as well as His forgiveness. I have heard women say, "But God doesn't care about me. He doesn't see how I'm being treated. He doesn't know what is happening to me." I've even heard some say, "God doesn't love me." And I've felt and said these things myself. Whenever we feel these things, we need to turn to the Bible and see the truth of God's love for us, His people.

When we open God's Word, we will see, for instance, how God cared for the Israelites. After Joseph died, the children of Israel were being mistreated by the new Pharaoh and felt—as perhaps you have—that God didn't care about them. The Book of Exodus, however, reports that this was never the case. God tells Moses that, even while the Israelites thought they were unloved and forgotten, He heard them, saw them, and took notice of their condition (2:24,25). Far from forgetting them, God remembered His covenant with them (2:24). At the burning bush, God added, "I have surely seen the affliction of my people. . . . I know their sorrows" (3:7 KJV). This true account reveals God's love by teaching that our God sees, hears, and knows the sufferings of His people. Our God also remembers His promises, cares about His people, and acts for their good. Regardless of life's circumstances, we must choose to think on these truths rather than yield to our own thoughts or feelings.

We also learn about God's love when we see in the Book of Genesis how He cared for Hagar, a favorite story of mine when I am tempted to think that God doesn't know or care about what is happening to me. Twice God met Hagar in times of distress. The first time she was pregnant and a fugitive, but "the angel of the Lord found her" and said, "The Lord hath heard thy affliction" (Genesis 16:7,11 KJV). After meeting God, Hagar referred to Him as "Thou art a God who sees" (verse 13), and her newborn son was named Ishmael, meaning "God hears" (verse 15).[4] Hagar recognized the truth that our God is a God who sees His people and hears their cries, and she experienced His care, concern, and provision.

Hagar's second encounter with God—sixteen years later—was also initiated by Him. Although time had passed, God still knew, saw, heard, cared, and provided for this single mother. After Abraham had sent Hagar and her son away and the two of them were dying in the desert, God heard the voice of the young man crying and provided them with water as well as encouragement (Genesis 21:1-19).

When I consider the God who heard, saw, knew, and rescued Hagar and the Israelites, my faith increases. Scenes like these from the Bible and the truth of 1 Peter 5:7 ("He cares for you") teach me that God cares about and for His people. And that is the kind of thought which honors God and enables us to rest in Him. We are loving God with all our mind when we rely on the powerful truths of His Word rather than on our own thoughts and feelings. We love God when we choose to submit our emotions and thoughts to the truth of His teachings.

Thinking About Ourselves

Just as Scripture can help us know God, it can also help us better know ourselves by showing us how God sees us. When we view ourselves through the lens of God's Word, we can replace self-defeating thought patterns with statements about His love for us and the worth we have in His eyes. The truth that Christ died for us (Romans 5:8), for example, tells us that we are valuable individuals even when we might not feel that we are. Such truth is key as we sift through our feelings to find the facts which Scripture teaches about our position before God in Christ. Truths like these as well as the Bible's guidelines for life enable us to experience the power of God rather than the draining effects of negative thoughts about ourselves.

I have to fight this battle against thinking negatively about myself every day, but one day recently the struggle was tougher than usual. I had accepted a writing assignment that challenged me to venture out beyond the safety zone of familiarity. Confident of God's leading, I tackled the assignment even though it was something I had never done before, and I worked harder and longer than ever—only to have my writing meet resistance and even rejection. I had failed.

Drained physically as well as emotionally, I crawled home to recover as these thoughts filled my mind: "Who do you think you are? You're nobody. You're nothing. When will you understand that the kind of ministry you were attempting is reserved for others better than you?" As the day went on, my thoughts became darker and darker. "Why don't you just quit now? Why try? Why care?" Finally I went for a walk. I had to get out of the house. But walking didn't help because, with each step up our huge hill, I continued to drill into my brain the chorus which had been there all day long.

But then the Holy Spirit broke through my relentless chant and prompted me to ask myself the key question— "Liz, what is true?" And the answers from Scripture which He brought to mind offered me peace and healing. He reminded me that I am fearfully and wonderfully made (Psalm 139:14), that He has a grand plan and purpose for my life (2 Timothy 1:9), and that He has given me spiritual gifts that I can use to benefit other believers (1 Corinthians 12:7). I also found comfort in the truth that, no matter what I experience, I am always loved and accepted by God (Romans 8:35). These thoughts were God's unshakable truth, and I found new strength in Him when He replaced the untrue thoughts that had been weighing me down with these precious facts about how He sees me.

Besides being prompted by life's disappointments and rejections, such untrue and debilitating thoughts about ourselves often arise from unmet expectations we have for ourselves. Too often we are unrealistic in the demands we make on ourselves. My dear friend Louise, for instance, suffers from the crippling effects of rheumatoid arthritis and has to constantly guard her expectations for herself. Her unending pain and fatigue tempt her to dwell on what she can't do or what she thinks she should be accomplishing. When that happens, Louise says, "It comforts me to remember that God is all-knowing and has a plan for me that includes my condition. I find rest as I trust in Him because He is faithful and will do what He promises."

When we think scripturally about ourselves and our circumstances, as Louise does, God uses His truth to break the cycle of destructive thinking that leads to discouragement, despair, doubt, and depression. However real the pain, the hurt, and the disappointments of life we may be experiencing, God gives us comfort, healing, and hope when His Spirit calls us to remember the greater reality of God's love, power, and redemption.

Whenever you find yourself thinking of yourself as useless or worthless, as a failure, a hopeless case, or a loser, remember what is true about you. As a Christian woman, you are a child of God (John 1:12) and His workmanship (Ephesians 2:10). You have been bought by the precious blood of Christ (1 Corinthians 6:20, 1 Peter 1:19). And when you and I love God with all our mind by thinking these true thoughts about ourselves, we can experience the joy and hope of being in relationship to God through Jesus Christ. With that joy comes fresh energy for life as the Holy Spirit uses God's Word to encourage us and enable us to live out His will for us.

Thinking About Relationships

Like our relationship with God and our perspective on ourselves, our relationships with people need to be guided by the command of Philippians 4:8 (KJV)— "Whatsoever things are true [real]...think on these things." Women who think on what is real do not spend time analyzing other people's words and actions or second-guessing what they say and do. Such negative thoughts damage relationships. When we focus on what is real, we experience sound and sincere relationships characterized by a genuine love for others.

Through the years, however, I have been guilty of playing mind-games with people and second-guessing their motives. It is all too easy to wonder about what a person isn't saying and to try to read between the lines of what he or she does say ("He says he loves me, but I don't think he does.. " and "He said there's nothing wrong, but I'm not sure...."). We come up with creative explanations for people's actions ("She's been grumpy lately, so she must be angry with me") and draw conclusions about why people do what they do ("She left a message on my machine to call her. I must have done something wrong" or "I wonder what she wants from me now"). We also apply this kind of thinking to what people do *not* do ("She hasn't called me in a while. I must have done something to offend her").

Two principles from Scripture can help settle a mind that is overly active when it comes to thinking about relationships. The first principle is based on 1 Corinthians 13, the apostle Paul's words about love. As he talks about love, Paul notes that love "thinketh no evil" and "believeth all things" (verses 5 and 7, KJV). I violate these two requirements for love whenever I question what another person says or does. My second-guessing involves interpreting and quite often distorting the words and actions of others. When I try to read into a person's words and actions rather than accepting what they say and do at face value, I am essentially making that person a liar. Instead, I need to stop my wild, speculative thoughts by asking myself, "But, Liz, what is true?" The answer to this question calls me to believe what the other person said.

Applying this principle of thinking no evil about another person and believing all that he or she has said eliminates second-guessing, reading between the lines, and the misunderstanding and hurt that can result. If he says he loves me, I believe that he loves me. If she says it doesn't matter, I believe that it doesn't matter. If he says nothing is wrong, I believe that nothing is wrong. I think on what is true. Such believing doesn't always come easily, though.

After a class on this principle from 1 Corinthians 13, one college student told me about trouble she had been having with a friend. "Even though this friend seems to be avoiding me and not talking to me as much as before," this woman wrote, "I'm trying not to assume anything. Instead, I'm praying about it and, as 1 Corinthians 13:7 says, believing the best. It's hard, though, because my mind almost automatically wants to assume the worst."

Another woman who had a similar experience was able to see progress. "When spending time with friends," she shared, "I found myself being too sensitive and taking things they did and said out of context. But I am learning to take things at face value and to distinguish between what is perceived and what is real."

Like her, you can break the habit of destructive thought patterns that damage relationships. Simply ask yourself, "What is true?" This can help stop the second-guessing, analysis, and introspection that hinder the development of healthy relationships. Accepting the words and actions of others at face value will also give you peace.

In Matthew 18:15, Jesus Himself offers a second principle for healthy relationships. He says, "If your brother sins, go and reprove him in private." The primary application of this truth is to simply obey the command. We are to go to any person who sins against us. But think about what this command means for you and me when other believers obey it, too. We can hope that, when we sin against other people, they will come to us in private to talk about it.

This truth has given me freedom. I no longer waste time and energy worrying about what other people think of me or what I do. I have stopped wondering what others might be thinking or what I might have done wrong. My guesses are just that. They're guesses rather than fact, reality, or truth. If people have been offended by something I've said or done, I rest in the fact that Matthew 18:15 instructs them to tell me. I also rest knowing that, in my times alone with the Lord, He can help me realize where I might have hurt or offended someone even if that person doesn't come to me. I trust that the Spirit of God will show me where I have fallen short in my relationships.

As I stopped analyzing my every move and second-guessing other people's ideas about me, I experienced more peace and greater openness in my relationships. I no longer fear or dread encounters with people, wondering what critical thoughts they might be thinking. Rather than looking for fault in things I've said or done, I now spend my energy on learning from God, through His Word, just what my attitudes and actions should be.

For me, the images of Proverbs 28:1 support this principle. The verse reads, "The wicked flee when no one is pursuing, but the righteous are bold as a lion." My paraphrase of this truth is "If you haven't done anything wrong, don't act like it!" We are to boldly and confidently proceed rather than holding back, wondering what people are thinking about us. This kind of going forward takes conscious effort, as one woman discovered: "A certain person was acting differently toward me. Normally I would have probed and speculated a lot, but I decided to act as if everything were okay. The next day she told me that she was dealing with some things and was sorry she had treated me badly. So [her behavior] wasn't because of something I had done after all."

What kinds of thoughts do you tend to have about people? I doubt that they are always pure, positive, and prayerful. Which one of us hasn't slipped into second-guessing, analysis, and suspicion? Which one of us hasn't been plagued by self-doubt or crippled by negative thoughts, insecurity, and worry? A woman choosing to think on what is true and real, however, depends on others to tell her and on God's Spirit to show her when she fails or offends someone. She refuses to second-guess or draw conclusions about people's behavior. When we think no evil about people, trust what they say and do, and believe that either they will come to us or God will reveal to us where we have offended them, we will nurture love and confidence in relationships. Thoughts about people, which are based on what is true and real, liberate us to generously and joyously love and serve one another.

The Power of God's Word

Clearly, the foundation for a healthy thought life is the Bible. God has chosen to communicate with us through the Bible, and therefore His Word is to take priority over all else we might choose as the basis of our thoughts, actions, and feelings. Furthermore, we come to know God Himself better through what the Bible reveals about Him. Through that revelation, God releases His power in our life, power which enables us to think radically different thoughts which will change our life and our conduct.

After all, the Word of God is designed to lead us to God, so thinking on His truth will mean being in closer relationship with Him. As we walk closely with Him, we will also experience His power in our life, power that can lift us out of the depths of defeat, discouragement, despair, doubt, dread, and depression and enable us to better deal with the challenges that come our way. With our thoughts based on the Word and Person of God and, therefore, our heart drawn closer to Him, we will find strength, hope, joy, faith, and peace of heart, soul, and mind. As we encounter the events life brings, we will experience victory. Freed from the crippling habits of our thought life, we will be able to move calmly and steadily forward with courage and confidence.

You and I can choose to think thoughts about God and life's situations which are not true, or we can choose to think the truths stated in Scripture. The story Ruth Graham tells about her parents, Dr. and Mrs. Nelson Bell, illustrates the power that comes with thinking biblical truths. Dr. and Mrs. Bell ministered in China for 20 years that were characterized by unrest and political and military upheaval. At one point, they lay in their dugout shelter, not knowing their fate. The situation appeared hopeless, and these missionaries could easily have been overwhelmed by panic and despair. The choice was theirs, and they chose to view their situation through the lens of God's truth.

Mrs. Bell reports: "We were counting over our defenses. . . . Overhead are the overshadowing wings

(Psalm 91:4); underneath are the everlasting arms (Deuteronomy 33:27); all around 'the angel of the Lord encampeth round about them that fear Him, and delivereth them,' (Psalm 34:7); inside, that 'Peace which passeth all understanding,' (Philippians 4:7); also, 'Thou wilt keep him in perfect peace, whose mind is stayed on Thee: because He trusteth in Thee' (Isaiah 26:3)."[5] The Bells' focus on God's truth enabled them to endure the challenges they faced.

And these same assurances which sustained Dr. and Mrs. Bell are available to you. The next time you feel yourself slipping from confidence to cowardice, from control to emotion, from the strength of spiritual mental health to frailty of spirit, review the resources you have as a child of God. In times of trauma and testing, choose to fill your mind with what is true. Choose to love God with all your mind.

No Longer a Prisoner

I'm glad my phone rang that morning so many years ago. With that woman's question, God prompted me to recall how He used His Word to help me overcome my struggle with depression, and that look back strengthened my commitment to know more of God's truth and to do exactly what it says.

As I remember the kind of woman I was and the kind of life I lived due to the thoughts that filled my mind, I am astonished. Having been a prisoner of dark moods generated by dark thoughts, I know all too well the frightening ability our thoughts have to program our lives. Scripture's analysis is true—"As [a man] thinks within himself, so he is" (Proverbs 23:7a).

As I look back, I am also overwhelmed with gratitude to God for His wisdom. Knowing the struggles His people would have, He provided help for us through His

Word. As we have seen, when the apostle Paul calls us in Philippians 4:8 to think on what is real, he is giving us what one commentator called a "paragraph on mental health."[6] While Paul's admonition is intended to help the church at Philippi deal with the problem of disunity, his words can also help each one of us develop a healthier thought life and experience the energy and effectiveness that come when we love God with all our mind. How thankful I am that God gave me this new insight into Philippians 4:8 when I needed it, and my prayer for myself is to love God more by knowing more of His Word and submitting more of my life to His truth.

Disciplining our thought life by focusing on God's true and reliable Word is a giant step toward truly experiencing the love of God so that we can love Him with all our mind. In the next chapter, we'll look at the Bible's guidelines for healthy thinking about the past, the future, and the challenges of the present.

2

Taking Every
Thought Captive

———— ❧ ————

Whatsoever things are true...
think on these things.
Philippians 4:8 (KJV)

———— ❧ ————

Whenever I teach or speak, I announce that I am
available afterwards for questions. One particular evening, a woman cautiously approached me. As
she began talking and well before she got to her question, I realized I was hearing someone talk about her
deepest fears.

I had very little eye contact with this woman whose
head hung so low. Her gripping fear constricted her
breathing, which explained the labored whisper. When
she did dare to look up, I saw intense pain in her eyes.
Hers was a face robbed of the smile lines God meant her
to have. Stress was taking its toll, and my heart ached for
this woman in her anguish. God's desire is that she
might live an abundant life (John 10:10), yet fear was
robbing her of joy, as it does many women.

Crippling Fear

Crippling fear comes to us for a variety of reasons. In
California where I live, for instance, *earthquakes* cause

women great concern. Many wives ask me about earthquakes when they first arrive at The Master's Seminary where my husband teaches. When newcomers to the state ask, "Liz, how do you know when you're having an earthquake? What does it feel like?" "Oh, you'll know when it happens," I say—and they do.

Finances, the prospect of *unemployment*, and the possibility of having to *return to work* also cause women worry and fear. Women who already have jobs because of money problems at home are afraid they will never get to stop working. Add the thoughts "I'm afraid we're going to lose our home" and "I'm afraid the economy will never improve," and it's easy to see how fear breeds more fear.

Every mother experiences fear for her *children*. During pregnancy, mothers fear for their baby's development and safe delivery. After they're born, babies bring money worries and the loss of a more carefree lifestyle. As the baby grows, fears increase as mothers worry about accidents, molestation, abuse, crime, violence, environmental pollution, and the future of the world. We women also wonder whether our children will come to love Christ and follow Him. Then, when our children are adults, we worry about their choice of a marriage partner, the new couple's finances, and possibility of divorce. When the grandchildren arrive, the cycle of fear begins anew.

Many career women fear a life of *singleness*. I remember a young woman at a singles' Bible study in our home. When Amy mentioned that the next meeting would be on her birthday, the group began planning a party for her. The plans were interrupted when Amy sobbed, "But you don't understand. This is not an occasion to celebrate. I'm going to be 30!" Her birthday would mean another year, another five years, another decade had passed—and she was still single.

Women who have been married fear the singleness of *divorce* and *widowhood*. During his ministry to senior citizens at our church, my husband regularly saw fear of *old age* and of needing convalescent care in later years and not being able to afford it. Many people—myself included—fear *illness and suffering*. I find great hope, however, when I watch my friend Allison who suffers from multiple sclerosis (MS). Our seminary wives' fellowship group prayed with her through the medical tests and the diagnosis, helplessly watched Allison struggle initially, and then tried to help as she began adjusting to a new kind of life.

One evening we wept together as Allison shared her thoughts on James 1:2-4. In that passage, James writes, "Consider it all joy, my brethren, when you encounter various trials, knowing that the testing of your faith produces endurance. And let endurance have its perfect result, that you may be perfect and complete, lacking in nothing." Months before she and her husband had come to the seminary, the women in her home church had studied James. Feeling stagnant as a Christian, Allison had read these first verses and prayed, "God, give me an opportunity to grow. Give me the opportunity to apply these truths in my life." Now, as she faced MS, Allison changed her prayer to, "God, give me joy in my trial." She began a "Journal of Joy" and one entry read, "God, I can have joy and thank You because my illness was not a brain tumor." Seeing how Allison deals with her illness reminds me that God is with us when we are sick, and my fear subsides.

Often closely related to the fear of illness is the fear of *death*. When will we die? How will we die? Will we suffer with dignity? Too rarely do we have the apostle Paul's perspective on death. In his letter to the Philippians, he says, "To die is gain" (1:21). He teaches that to die is simply "to depart and to be with Christ" (1:23) and that to be with Christ "is very much better" (1:23). As an unknown poet wrote, "Better, far better, with Christ to be, living and loved through eternity."

Perhaps you can add your own fears to this list—and perhaps, having read chapter 1, you have an idea of how God can use His truth in your life to help you, whatever your fears.

Overcoming Fear

What can we do to overcome our fears? How can we keep fear from robbing today of its joys? What can we do to control this raging and damaging emotion? How can we stop thinking these thoughts that hurt us? Again, Philippians 4:8 offers us a clue. Consider that fear is rooted in thoughts about things that are not real and remember the admonition of Philippians 4:8 (KJV)— "Whatsoever things are true [or real]...think on these things."

As we saw in the preceding chapter, the first few words of Philippians 4:8 challenge us to think on what is true or real and to function according to facts, not feelings or fantasies. What we think must be true according to what the Bible says, true according to the character of God as revealed in the Bible, and true according to what people say and do. As God uses His Word in our life and enables us to think on what is real, He calms our fears about the future, the past, and the present.

Thinking about the Future

Do you frequently find yourself asking the question, "What if...?" That question has the ability to generate all kinds of fear about the future. Philippians 4:8, however, teaches that our thoughts should "belong to the nature of reality,"[1] a guideline which rules out any fearful dwelling on the future. Philippians 4:8 commands us to think on what is true and real, and events in the future are neither. Philippians 4:8 is, therefore, a challenge to learn not to probe the future with fear-generating questions like "What if I never get married?" "What if I lose my husband?" "What if I get cancer?" and "What if my children rebel?" Questions like that can too easily fill our mind and keep us from loving God as He calls us to do. That was the case with Patty, whom I met at a women's retreat.

As I spoke, I spotted Patty's distraught face in the audience. At one of the breaks, she came up to me and explained that she and her husband had wanted a baby for more than ten years. They were thrilled when God blessed them with a baby—but now it was time for the baby's DPT immunization. Having read about the mortality rate linked to DPT shots, this mother was postponing the shot. She voiced her fear to me—"What if my baby dies from that injection?"

Whatever our "what if," we need to remember that "what if" is a guess. If we want to overcome our fears, we cannot think "what if." Instead, in obedience to Philippians 4:8, we have to acknowledge that events in the future are not real and eliminate this kind of speculative thinking. Thoughts about the future are, at best, only guesses. Furthermore, the future is in God's hands, His loving, capable, merciful, powerful hands. He can enable us to deal with what is real, with what is now, and He will be with us whatever the future holds (Matthew 28:20). While we need to be prepared for things like earthquakes and we need to be wise about our finances, our parenting, and our health, we don't need to waste energy worrying about what is not yet real and therefore may never come to pass.

Consider again, item by item, the list of fears we looked at. Each one was a "what if" concern. Not one event was real. Not one event had actually happened. Possible earthquakes, the first item on the list, exist only in the mind. Likewise, potential money problems aren't today's money problems. Similarly, a mother's worries about the future are not real. We parents are to focus our energy on what we do today because today is real. God asks mothers to nurture, train, and discipline their children today (Ephesians 6:4) and then wake up tomorrow and do the same thing. Being overly concerned about potential parenting problems in the future will sap our energy and our joy and interfere with our efforts as parents today. God calls us to handle each day one at a time. Today is real, and God will enable us to deal with what today holds.

That same principle holds for single women. God does not ask single women to look down through the corridors of time and imagine that they will be single forever. Again, He calls a single woman to address what is real, and what is real is her singleness today. Although her desire may be to be married, she—like all of us— would do well to heed the wise words of missionary Jim Elliot. While waiting on God's will regarding marriage, Jim Elliot wrote to his future wife, Elisabeth Howard, "Let not our longing slay the appetite of our living."[2] Commenting on this wisdom decades later, Mrs. Elliot wrote, "We accept and thank God for what is given, not allowing the NOT-GIVEN to spoil it."[3] God is adequate.

Next in the list of fears was widowhood. Even though widowhood is a possibility, God does not want a married woman to ruin today's joy with her husband by entertaining the thought of his death. God promises that, when the actuality comes, He will be "a judge for the widows" (Psalm 68:5) and will "establish the boundary of the widow" (Proverbs 15:25). God also offers His presence and provision to those who fear old age with the promise, "Even to your old age... and even to your graying years I shall bear you.... I shall carry you" (Isaiah 46:4). God will take care of you and me in our later years. God is and will be sufficient.

Moving through our list, we see that God also does not want our fear of possible illness and suffering to overshadow the reality of our usefulness and health today. If we someday find ourselves experiencing physical trials, God will be with us through them, and we will find, with Paul, that "I can do all things through Him who strengthens me" (Philippians 4:13). God will strengthen.

Finally, the fear of death—the ultimate reality for all of us—can keep us from living a full and productive life. But we can surrender that fear to God's promise that He will be with us even "through the valley of the shadow of death" (Psalm 23:4). God is and will be present with us.

You may have noticed a pattern in these suggestions about how to deal with "what if" fears. The way to let go of those fears is to draw close to God and acknowledge His presence, His power, and His love. "What if" questions fail to acknowledge God. We therefore need to turn to His Word and be reminded of the many promises that "God is with you wherever you go" (Joshua 1:9). Our God is the God of the past, the present, and the future. He has promised to guide you throughout your life and receive you to glory afterward (Psalm 73:24). Like David, we can be sure that "goodness and lovingkindness will follow me all the days of my life, and I will dwell in the house of the Lord forever" (Psalm 23:6).

We experience peace instead of worry when we choose to believe the Scripture's promises that God will superintend every future event. Nothing will ever happen to you that God does not already know about. Nothing will ever happen to you that is a mistake (Psalm 139:4,16). Nothing will ever happen that you cannot handle by God's power and grace (2 Corinthians 12:9-10). Nothing will ever happen to you that will not eventually be used by God for some good purpose in your life (Romans 8:28-29). And nothing will ever happen to you apart from God's presence (Matthew 28:20).

We need to remember that the future is not real. The future exists only in our imagination. We will deal with tomorrow . . . tomorrow when it is present and real. Yes, we need to plan for the future and set goals for ourselves, but we suffer when we worry about things which might happen. Having planned for the future as best we can and then leaving it in God's hands, we do better when we use most of our energy to draw close to God in the present and to think about and deal with things that are real.

Thinking About the Past

Like our "what if" thoughts about the future, our "if only" thoughts about the past can rob us of peace and joy in the present. Paul exhorts us in Philippians 4:8 (KJV) to think on "whatsoever things are true [or real]," and the past is no more real than the future. I know firsthand how tightly we can be gripped by the habit of looking backward to events in the past and thinking, "If only I had done that differently," "If only I hadn't done that," "If only that hadn't happened," or "If only I had been better informed."

For years after I became a Christian, I struggled with the thought, "If only I had become a Christian sooner!" After all, I reasoned, coming to Christ sooner would have meant helpful guidelines for our marriage and a sure foundation for raising our two daughters. Our eight years of marriage before we knew Christ were rough, and adding two children hadn't helped as we continued living apart from God and His direction for our lives. When Christ entered our home, however, and we read God's Word, His Spirit opened our eyes to what we had been doing wrong and showed us how to live as God would have us live. Also, when I was a new Christian, I realized that I had lived for myself and so had missed out on some precious opportunities and important years of nurturing my daughters. "If only I had become a Christian sooner, I would have been a better wife, I would have been a better mother, I would have had Christ's love to share in my own home, and I would have known to serve and sacrifice instead of being so self-serving. If only..."

The Holy Spirit, however, used certain questions to turn me away from these "if only" thoughts and point me toward the Sovereign God who, after all, was in control of my salvation and my life. He asked me, "Liz, who was in charge of your salvation? Who picked the exact day and minute? Who knew from before time when you would believe in Jesus? Who knew about the two little girls and their needs? Who handpicked you to be their mother? Who used a rocky marriage and an unfulfilling family life to open your eyes to your needs?" At this point, I was on my knees in adoration of God, the One who controlled and controls my life. He knew how my life would unfold, when I would come to know Him, and how I would come to serve Him. This is what is true and real and far more important than my "if only..." daydreams.

Jenny, a woman I sat next to at a seminary wives' luncheon, also knew the struggle with "if only" thinking. The women at the luncheon were sharing how their husbands had come to attend seminary. A common feature of many of the stories was meeting and marrying in college. Jenny, the last one to share, lamented, "I feel left out here today. If only I had gone to college...." But when I finished teaching about thinking on what is real and not on "if only," Jenny smiled and whispered to me, "Wow, I'll sure never say that again! Thanks!"

God had directed Jenny's past and brought her and her husband together even though they didn't go to college together. God is also able to use Jenny mightily even though she doesn't have a college education. These facts are true and real. Jenny's "if only" thinking was unnecessary interference which held her back by fostering feelings of inferiority and regret.

Such "if only" thinking is counterproductive, first, because it doesn't address what is real. The past is gone. It is beyond repair or restructuring. What is real is what is happening today, and God calls us to deal with what is now. Second, as we've seen in Jenny and perhaps as you yourself have experienced, "if only" thinking breeds remorse. The backward gaze can produce regret and sorrow. It is impossible to return to the past, so what value is there to rehashing it?

Rehashing the past, however, is quite different from remembering in obedience to Scripture's instruction. Remembering the past is of immeasurable value when we learn from our mistakes and recall God's marvelous works and gracious faithfulness to us. It's important to look back to see how God enabled us in our times of need and how He brought us through our trials. We need to look back and see what God has taught us on the mountains and in the valleys of life. Like the writer of Psalm 77, we are to meditate on God's goodness in the past when the trials of the present seem overwhelming: "I shall remember the deeds of the Lord; surely I will remember Thy wonders of old" (verse 11). We are to remember God's faithfulness to us when we look back at the past, an act of remembrance quite different from the "if only" mentality.

Focusing like this on God's faithfulness to us in the past counters our failure to acknowledge God's role in our past. When we succumb to "if only" thinking, we are ignoring the fact that God was there with us. He was with you then just as He is with you today and will be with you tomorrow (Psalm 73:23-24). Acknowledging God's sovereignty over every event of your life—past, present, and future—is a vital step toward experiencing His love and toward responding by loving Him with all your mind. As the Supreme Ruler and One who is omni-present through time, God knew the events of your life before the foundation of the world (Ephesians 2:10; 2 Timothy 1:9). He knew each detail of the path your life would take. He has allowed your life to unfold as it has, and He has overseen all that has happened to you. He has been present with you and involved in your life as His plan for you has unfolded. He could have planned your life differently, but He didn't. Let this mysterious and wondrous truth help you look back through eyes of faith and without regret or remorse.

If we look back at the past without trusting that God was there with us, we sentence ourselves to a life of regret, and that is what one missionary couple Jim and I met in the Philippines seemed to be doing. When it was time for their oldest child to start school, they enrolled her in a Christian boarding school. At the end of that first year, the little girl told her parents about her loneliness and tears. At that moment, they concluded that they had made a horrible mistake.

My husband listened to their story and then asked, "Did you pray before you decided to send your daughter to boarding school?" Devoted Christians and devoted parents, they had indeed prayed. Jim then asked, "Did you seek wise counsel before you decided to send her to boarding school?" Again, the answer was yes. Gently, Jim asked, "Do you think that, after you prayed and sought wise counsel, your decision really could have been a horrible mistake?" What joy it was for us to watch their faces as, for the first time, they looked back at their experience through the eyes of faith. Their "if only" thinking had kept them from remembering their decision-making process. A burden was lifted from them and they found real relief as they recalled how they had sought God's guidance each step of the way. As hard as that year must have been on their daughter, they could trust that God had been present with her and that He would use that hard time for her good.

As the God of the past, our heavenly Father does indeed use our past. The great truth of Romans 8:28-29 is God's promise that any and all events in the past will be worked for good to make you more like Christ. He will redeem even the worst, the most painful, and the most perplexing aspects of your past and use it all for some good. I have seen God redeem the suffering and terrible trials in many people's lives. In fact, some of the women I know who extend most freely God's gentleness, peace, and grace to those around them are women who know pain. God has used their experiences to make these women more Christlike, and He is truly glorified in their lives.

So the next time you catch yourself saying or thinking "if only," I encourage you to pause and ponder the fact of God's sovereignty, knowledge, and presence in that past situation. Refuse to allow yourself to get bogged down thinking about something that is no longer real. Instead, draw near to God by thanking Him for His continual presence with you throughout time and for His promise to redeem the hard times of the past.

Thinking About the Present

Just as we need to follow the exhortation of Philippians 4:8 as we consider the future and the past, we need to think on what is true and real in the present—and, as I know from experience, that is not always easy to do.

As a young mother, I chose Proverbs 22:6 ("Train up a child in the way he should go, even when he is old he will not depart from it") as a guiding Scripture for raising my children. Holding tightly to this promise, I began to train my children in the way they "should go." A decade later, however, my mothering didn't seem to be working. I wasn't seeing the results I had expected. Angry, I said to God, "But this isn't the way it was supposed to be! This isn't the way it went for this family here or that family over there, and this isn't the way it was supposed to be for my family." Like a child who didn't get what she wanted, I threw a tantrum and spent my time and energy kicking, screaming, and battling God. Then, one day, when I finally took a breath during my rantings to listen, God seemed to say, "But, Liz, this is the way it is. Now what are you going to do about it?" Again like a child, I realized I had to quit yelling, get up, and go on, so I did.

I was forced to face reality. Because of my unmet expectations, I had been postponing any action. Because I didn't like what I saw, I was failing to do anything to try to improve the situation. I wasn't dealing with the circumstances and I wasn't prepared to because this was not the way it was supposed to be. As long as I had that attitude—as long as I didn't accept reality—no progress or solution was possible. As long as I wished for reality to be different, I failed to handle the problem.

I know many women who refuse to face reality when it comes to their marriage. Our fantasies, expectations, and dreams about what marriage will be are usually quite different from the reality. When that reality sets in, many women are stunned into immobility. Unhappy, they say to me, "I don't know why I ever married him in the first place—and I wish I hadn't!" As their counselor, I say, "But this is the way it is. Now, what are you going to do about this reality?" Once we accept reality—the reality of our marriage, our family, our job, whatever—we can use our energy to make that reality better.

Our assignment is to accept what is real. We are to acknowledge that God oversees and has overseen every detail of our lives—our singleness, our marriage, our family, our job, every situation and every circumstance every day. This knowledge can help us—with faith, with hope, and with Him by our side—act on what is real today rather than resent reality and idly wait for fantasies to somehow materialize.

Training Your Thoughts

So what can you and I do to develop the kind of thinking that leads to loving God with all our mind? How can we begin to focus our mental energy on present realities? How can we discipline ourselves to stop thinking along the futile and destructive paths of "what if" and "if only"? The key is our relationship with God and the power He gives us to do all that He calls us to do. The following three steps have helped me and many others draw closer to God and develop thought patterns which reflect His truth. I encourage you to try them yourself.

Step 1: Recognize the Command—In Philippians 4:8, Paul commands us to think on what is real. He is not making a suggestion or offering a piece of advice which we can take or leave. Philippians 4:8 is God's command to us to focus our thoughts on the truth of His Word and the things in life that are real.

What has helped me in my efforts to obey this command is the awareness that to disobey God's command is to sin. "If the Bible says I can only think on what is true and what is real," I reasoned, "to think outside of those biblical boundaries is sin." Labeling thoughts that were not based on what is true or real as sin was a great motivator for me. Wanting to obey God's Word, I sought to have my every thought measure up to God's standard of true or real. My thinking was either based on that truth or it wasn't. My thinking was either right or wrong; it was either acceptable or sinful. I felt I had to be this rigid if I were, in obedience to God's command, to let go of my destructive thought patterns and think on what is real.

Equally important, though, is my awareness of God's grace. Yes, to disobey any of His commands is sin, but we don't have to rely on our own efforts to respond in obedience. Instead, God is at work to help us accomplish all that He calls us to do. Our ability to obey any and all of His commands—including the command to think on what is true—comes from Him. He enables us to love Him with our whole mind.

Step 2: Respond in Obedience—Having acknowledged that Philippians 4:8 is one of God's commands, I began to wonder what I could do to obey it. How could I limit my thinking to what is true or real? I found a clue from Paul himself in 2 Corinthians 10:5 where he writes, "We are destroying speculations and every lofty thing raised up against the knowledge of God, and we are taking every thought captive to the obedience of Christ." By definition, thoughts that are not true or real are mere "speculations." They are "lofty things raised up against the knowledge of God," and they have to be taken "captive to the obedience of Christ."

The image that came to mind as I considered taking my thoughts captive to Christ came from my childhood in a tiny Oklahoma town. It was a grand occasion each year when our family attended the local rodeo, and the calf roping was a highlight. Ready on his horse and with his lasso in hand, a cowboy waited for a calf to be released from its chute. Then came the chase as the cowboy went after the bucking, twisting, running animal, lassoed it, brought it in, jumped off his horse, threw the calf down with both hands, tied three legs together, jumped up, and raised his hand in victory. The timer stopped. The cowboy had successfully roped the calf.

I realized I needed to be like that cowboy as I handled any thoughts that were not true or real. My "what if" and "if only" thoughts were untamed and rebellious, bucking, jumping, wanting attention, and running wild in my mind. Like the cowboy—and with God's help—I needed to chase after them, rope them, bring them in, throw them on the ground, and use both hands to tie them down.

Taking our thoughts captive to Christ—to the Word of God, to what is true and real—calls for energy and effort. As the editors of the New English Bible put it, we must "compel every human thought to surrender to the obedience of Christ."[4] But this battle—a battle *in* the mind and a battle *for* the mind—is a battle we fight sustained by God's grace and empowered by His love. We don't change ourselves or our thinking by our own power. As we draw closer to Him, though, we experience His transforming presence and freedom from thoughts which do not honor Him.

Step 3: Reap the Benefits—When we acknowledge God's command and take steps to obey it, we will find ourselves enjoying greater energy and spending less time in melancholy introspection. Thinking thoughts that are true and real frees up our energy for positive uses and constructive purposes.

Not only have I experienced this myself, but I witness it often. I see it in women I meet who, new to California, spend their energy thinking about where they used to live (which is no longer true or real) and, consequently, feeling sad and bitter where they do live (which is true and real). Many women I've met waste time and energy reminiscing about the good ol' days and let today slip by. Others are consumed by thoughts of where they wish they were, what they want to have, what could have been, or what they might have done. When we choose this kind of thinking, real life slips by, unused and unenjoyed. Futile thoughts like these drain our precious energy. We waste it on what is false and what is fantasy.

For a moment, think of your Christian life as a bucket which God wants to fill so that He can use your life to glorify Him and enrich the lives of others. Reading the Bible every day is one way of filling that bucket, and thinking wrong thoughts (holding inaccurate ideas about God, other people, and God's Word as well as dwelling on "what if" and "if only" scenarios) is one way of draining it. Thoughts about things that are untrue and unreal will drain our life and our energy. Obeying the command of Philippians 4:8, however, helps keep our bucket full and our energy available to serve God. Thinking on what is true and real frees us to be used by God.

So how do we love God with all our mind? We choose to trust what the Bible reveals about God and ask Him to replace any fears and doubts with the truth of His Word. What the Bible teaches about God—about His love, wisdom, power, redemption, healing, patience, forgiveness, and ultimate victory—speaks directly to our concerns about the past, the present, and the future because it speaks to us of God's constant and unconditional love for us.

Furthermore, knowing what God's Word says about the past can free us from that past. The past has made us who we are, and we need to learn from the past. But dwelling on the unchangeable past can sap us of energy and deprive us of much joy. Said positively, knowing that God is the God of our past and trusting it to Him can free us to enjoy life in the present.

Finally, life is difficult and bad things do happen to good people, but when we know the truth of Scripture, we can lay before God the hurts, the tragedies, and the challenges we face. Instead of dwelling on our problems, we can choose to think about God's ability to handle those problems. Even as we feel the pain that life brings our way, we can experience the peace which passes understanding, the peace which God gives His people (Philippians 4:7). Such promises from Scripture can be the source of much comfort, hope, and peace when we choose to think about those realities as we deal with the difficult circumstances of life.

In Philippians 4:8, God commands us to think on what is true and real. When we think on God's truth and His love for us, He frees us from fear and regret, two major robbers of the energy and confidence necessary for dealing with life today. When we take our thoughts captive to Christ, we see Him hanging on the cross for our sins. This powerful image reminds us of God's great love for us and compels us to love Him in return with all our heart, all our soul, and all our mind.

3

Winning Over
Worry

———— ❧ ————

Do not be anxious for tomorrow;
for tomorrow will care for itself.
Each day has enough trouble of its own.
Matthew 6:34

———— ❧ ————

The first sound I heard was the blaring alarm clock. Despite the fog of disturbed sleep, I managed to hit the snooze button. I slept deeply through the first nine-minute interval. During the next snooze period, however, my mind moved quickly from barely functioning to worrying to panic.

"Oh, no! Another day, another thousand things to do!" The panic had begun. This bright, fresh day was a gift from God, and I wanted to say with the psalmist, "This is the day which the LORD hath made; Let us rejoice and be glad in it" (Psalm 118:24), but I couldn't. I was too overwhelmed by the mountain range of responsibility that comprised my life. Doing all I needed to do that day seemed impossible. My list was long, my schedule was full, and my calendar was booked. People, commitments, deadlines, housework, errands, needs—my list seemed endless. And, on occasion, yours probably does, too. Life is crowded, complex, and challenging. There is always so much to do.

In Matthew 6:34, however, Jesus speaks to this too-common feeling of being overwhelmed by life. He says to you and to me, "Do not be anxious for tomorrow; for tomorrow will care for itself. Each day has enough trouble of its own." With these words of common-sense wisdom, Jesus reduces our responsibilities to those of today. He forces our focus from the panorama view of the mountain range of forever to the single mountain of today. Today is all Christ asks us to manage, and today is something Christ knows we—with His help—can indeed manage. His words give me hope, and His words give me focus.

Matthew 6:34 includes Christ's command ("Do not be anxious for tomorrow"), His insight ("Tomorrow will care for itself"), and His challenge for us today ("Each day has enough trouble of its own"). He calls us away from worrying about tomorrow—a major contributor to stress—to addressing the reality of today. His job assignment for us is "Deal with today," and, as is the case for all that God commands us, He works in our life and in our heart to enable us to obey Him. The following five very practical guidelines also help me focus on today and on God's presence with me. With that focus, I am more able to love God with all my mind even as I go about meeting the nuts-and-bolts practical demands of the day (the topic of this chapter) as well as its emotional, physical, and mental demands (the topic of the next chapter).

Guideline #1: Prepare

Prepare in the evening. If you were going to climb a mountain early tomorrow morning, you would do certain tasks the night before. A woman who feels overwhelmed by all the demands on her does well to follow that same principle: Do certain tasks the night before.

Look at tomorrow's calendar. What is scheduled? What is happening in each family member's life? What is planned for dinner? Prepare as much of tomorrow's evening meal as possible (make the jello, cook the potatoes for potato salad, brown the chicken pieces, wash and tear the lettuce, chop the vegetables, assemble the casserole, etc.). While you're in the kitchen, prepare tomorrow's lunches and set the table for the next meal. Clean up the kitchen and run the dishwasher. Nothing starts my day better than an orderly and spotless kitchen.

Before you go to bed, take a few minutes to tidy the house. Again, the neatness will be a blessing in the morning. Also, lay out clothes for tomorrow so you won't have to think about what to wear in the morning. Before you turn out the lights, put by the door anything you'll need for tomorrow (lunches, briefcases, the dry cleaning, schoolbags, coats, purse, keys, mail, packages, etc.). Then, as you go to bed, be sure that the alarm is set so that you have enough time to do what needs to be done in the morning.

Prepare in the morning. The first step we take is important because it sets the tone for the day, and I've found that getting up when the alarm goes off puts me in control of my day. Hitting the snooze alarm too many times puts me in a game of catch-up—and that snooze alarm may be doing the same for you.

Once we're up, we need spiritual input for the day. Jesus Himself knew the value of an early-morning meeting with the Father. We read in Mark 1:35 that "in the early morning, while it was still dark, He arose and went out and departed to a lonely place, and was praying there." The day before, Jesus had preached, cast out demons, and healed people. Even after sundown, He had "healed many who were ill with various diseases, and cast out many demons" (verse 34). Then, early the next morning, Jesus arose for time with His Father so He would be refreshed and refilled for another day of ministry.

Perhaps true to your experience, however, Jesus' time alone with God was interrupted. Simon Peter and his friends approached Him, saying, "Everyone is looking for You" (Mark 1:37). Do you ever feel as if everyone is looking for you? Do you sometimes feel that everyone needs something from you? With people depending on you, you may have very few moments alone, and even then you may feel that you're "on call." Jesus knows what it's like to have people clamoring after Him for what only He can give. But one writer points out that, although "Christ's life was surrounded by hurricane-like winds and forces . . . they never deterred Him from His priorities or His sense of mission! He was never unnerved and never responded in a way that was out of line with His character."[1] Jesus remained focused in His work and loving toward people because, the writer continues, He spent time with His Father, "a time of restorative withdrawal . . . [where] energies are renewed, perspectives refocused, and directions newly defined."[2]

If you're like me, you may find that your most harried days are those days when you have failed to make time with Christ. As another woman puts it, "Put Christ off, [and] the result is frequently exhaustion (both physical and spiritual), loss of perspective, defensiveness, self-pity, and an absence of joy. . . . We become sapped. With [Christ] we seem tireless by contrast."[3] Is that your experience? Like Jesus Himself, we do well to first withdraw from the people who need us so that we will be able to serve them later. Like Jesus, we will be more ready to give to them when we ourselves have already received from the Father the guidance, perspective, strength, and grace we need for the day.

When the disciples found Jesus and told Him of all the people who needed Him, Christ confidently said, "Let us go somewhere else to the towns nearby, in order that I may preach there also; for that is what I came out for" (Mark 1:38). He had obtained His orders for the day, and obeying them took priority over the seemingly urgent needs of the crowds the disciples knew about. Again, we who may easily fall into the trap of other people's plans for us or the tyranny of the urgent can learn from Christ's example here. In His quiet time alone with God before the sun arose, Jesus acquired His focus for the day and He let it shape His plans.

You and I endanger our health, our service to others, and our relationship with God when we don't take time to be alone with Him. In fact, as one woman puts it, "Without large blocks of silence and solitude . . . we are in danger of losing the very best things that people desire to draw from us."[4] Alone with God, during some moments of stillness which are quite different from the activities and busyness of the rest of the day, we receive what people need us to give to them. Then, by the time "everyone is looking for you"—by the time the family gets up, the phone rings, or you get into the car—you have God's direction for your day.

With our mind focused right from the start on God's daily assignment to us, we are better able to receive His love throughout the day and love Him in return. His perspective on our responsibilities and His ordering of the day's activities will enable us to climb the mountain. When you and I start the day reminded of God's love for us, we are better prepared to meet the challenges that await, including the challenge of loving God through it all.

Guideline #2: Plan Ahead

Like preparing ahead of time, planning ahead also helps us be more effective during the course of our day, and our planning needs to be both long-range and short-range. Long-range planning is key to birthday celebrations, weddings, reunions, parties, vacations, and trips.

Papers, articles, theses, and dissertations require the same long-range planning as do redecorating, adding on to your house, or building a new one. We also need to plan ahead for buying or selling a home, moving, and retirement.

With long-range planning, we break large projects into day-sized pieces, an approach which can keep us from feeling overwhelmed by the ultimate goal and focused on today. I learned this lesson well in my own living room when it came time to hang new wallpaper. My husband and I had the paper and equipment we needed, but we didn't have a weekend or even a single, completely open day to do the job. Standing in the middle of the living room, I sobbed, "We'll never get this done. We just don't have time to do this. We'll get all the stuff out, make a big mess, and then have to put it all away. There's no way to get this done."

I remember Jim's next words now, more than twenty years later: "Liz, how do you eat an elephant?" After I whimpered, "I don't know," Jim said, "You eat an elephant one bite at a time. We're going to get the stuff out, we're going to cut the first strip, we're going to put it on the wall, and then we'll put it all away, but we will have taken the first bite." Acting on this elephant principle, we took the first step and made some progress.

With long-range planning, large and long-term projects are broken down into small tasks. We deal effectively with the future by taking care of the manageable pieces of the present's daily tasks. We don't waste precious energy on worry, fear, panic, or dread of the future. When we plan ahead, we feel more capable of meeting life's challenges and reaching life's goals.

Planning ahead in the short-term also enables us to better meet the day's demands. For me, lists are key. I make a "to do" list for work tasks, a grocery list for my shopping trips, and errand lists for when I'm out and about. I include on my lists tasks from my long-range planning as well as those day-to-day items which are part of keeping a home going. Once I look at my lists, I schedule when I will do each job. Lists and a schedule help me get the work done.

Janelle told me how lists helped her deal with an especially stressful time in her life. She was expecting a baby any time, remodeling her house, and fighting the cleaning problems the construction created. Her solution was planning: "I sat down and wrote out all the projects under three headings—baby, remodel, general cleaning. I have been able to plan each day by selecting one or two things from each heading to get done that day. This has helped immensely. Instead of one huge to-do list, that I know will never get done before the baby arrives, I've been able to put things into manageable bites—and by God's grace, I'm making headway!"

A plan, a schedule, and Matthew 6:34 to remind you not to be anxious can help you enjoy a productive day characterized by closeness with the Lord and free of frustration, anxiety, and their effects on your life.

Guideline #3: Pray

As we prepare and plan, we need to also be praying. Each day, I try to make the following three points part of my prayers. First, I give God everything, and I begin by giving God myself. British preacher and writer F. B. Meyer had seven rules to live by every day. Number one on his list was "Make a daily, definite, audible consecration of yourself to God. Say it out loud: Lord, today I give myself anew to you."[5] When I give myself to God like this, I find relief and peace. This fresh commitment reminds me that, as God's child, I belong to Him. As a bookmarker in my Bible says, "God is ready to assume full responsibility for the life wholly yielded to Him."

I also give God the things in my life—my home, my

_____

possessions, my time, my body, and my mind. These words of dedication remind me of my role as God's steward. God has given me everything I have, and I am to care for them and use them in ways that please Him.

Finally I give God the people in my life—my husband, my children, and my family members. My love is fierce when it comes to these precious people, but giving them to God calms the thoughts and quiets the worries. After all, our God is wise, powerful, loving, and able to take care of the people as well as the things in our life. I need to acknowledge His ability, and when I do so, I experience His peace.

Giving God everything means giving Him myself, my things, and the people I care about as well as the physical, the practical, and the emotional concerns of my life. All of these are His to do with as He likes. This complete commitment to God of all that I am and all that I have is another way I respond to God's love and try to love Him with all my mind—and making this commitment daily is key.

Second, after giving God everything, I give God Plan A for the day. Giving God my schedule for the day means laying before Him all of the projects I want to get done. Committing my plans to God through prayer helps me fight a better battle against impulsiveness and laziness. It also helps me be more sensitive to His leading me to do something other than what I have planned— which brings me to the third point in my daily prayers. I give God Plan B for the day. Wanting my plan to be His plan for me, I commit my day, my goals, and my energies to Him. Although I have a plan, I want God's will for my life. I therefore hold my plan loosely and stand ready to defer to what He would have me doing during the course of the day.

The perspective which comes with this surrendering my agenda to God reduces my frustration. I make Plan A and submit it to God. But when I give Him Plan B, I am acknowledging His right to create an alternative plan for my day. I try to approach each day thinking, "Plan A is good unless God moves me to Plan B. Then Plan B is better because Plan B is God's plan." Realizing that God is behind any unexpected event, I can then more easily accept whatever happens. When God reveals His will through Plan B, I want to accept it as His will.

Besides helping reduce my frustration when my plans change, giving God Plan B also helps me be more flexible. Pastor Ray Ortlund's example greatly encourages me: "I like to start out the morning covering my whole day by prayer. . . . I take out my appointment book and pray through the hours. I pray for everyone I am scheduled to see. . . . I pray for the unscheduled ones I will bump into. I've found that if I pray over my interruptions and get them squarely under God's sovereign control, they don't irritate me. I realize that they are part of God's plan."[6] We are to make a plan for the day, pray over that plan, and then proceed with that plan. When we are willing to regard the unexpected as God's intervention, we can flex with the new plan, recognizing it as God's plan.

Giving God Plan B like this greatly improves my attitude as I start my day. Having given God my day, I can then say, "Okay, God, let's see what's going to happen. Let's see where this day goes." This outlook creates in me an attitude of expectancy and acceptance. I look forward to seeing God at work in my life even when His plan is quite different from my plans.

I remember reading about Thomas Edison's reaction as his laboratories were burning and his life's work was going up in flames. He exclaimed, "Son, go get your mother quick! She's never seen a fire like this!" When looking over the smoldering ruins the next morning, he was able to say, "Just think. All our mistakes have been burned up and we have a chance to start all over again."[7] May I have that attitude when my plans seem to be up in smoke! May I be glad for the chance to do what God would have me do!

In obedience to Jesus' command in Matthew 6:34, we are to focus on today, and prayer can help us do just that. Through prayer, we can cast all our anxieties upon God (1 Peter 5:7), give Him everything (including Plan A and Plan B for the day), and experience the peace, focus, wisdom, and strength He would give us for the day. After all, He is the One who enables us to meet Christ's challenge to deal with today's "trouble" and today's trouble only.

Guideline #4: Proceed

Preparing, planning, and praying move us to the base of the mountain of today. Now it is time to begin the climb. Ancient wisdom reminds us that a journey of a thousand miles begins with a single step, and that truth can help us tackle the day one step at a time, one task at a time, one minute at a time. And we can take each of those steps, in obedience to Matthew 6:34, without worry.

In writing about Jesus' command to put off tomorrow's anxiety until tomorrow, one commentator observed, "If this be done, the greater part of all our anxiety is put aside at once, and for the rest of it, the principle will apply to each hour as well as to each day."[8] In other words, not only do we not need to worry about tomorrow, but we also don't need to worry about the next hour. We don't need to worry about interruptions because they are one way God reveals His will for our day. This perspective enables us to focus on the task at hand. When it is time, we'll take the next step and do the next task, refusing to worry about what lies ahead.

As you proceed with your plan and remain open to

God's plan, you will find yourself walking with God through the day and not worrying about tomorrow. That's obedience to the command of Matthew 6:34. You've prepared for the day, made your plans, and lifted them before God in prayer. Now live this day fully by experiencing the joy of the Lord, walking with Him as you go from task to task, meeting the needs of your husband, children, and others, and handling whatever God brings—and doing all this in His power and without anxiety. Then wake up tomorrow and do it again. As C. S. Lewis wrote, "Relying on God has to begin all over again every day as if nothing yet had been done."[9]

As I've worked on focusing on today and looking to God for strength and guidance, I've realized that my approach to life is much like my approach to running. I plan and prepare at home. Once I have on the right clothes and the right shoes, it's time to run. I run to the first corner and then to the next corner. But as the run gets longer and I get tired, I run not to the next corner but to the trash can I see, to a certain curb, to the next driveway, to the stoplight. As I get closer to home, I concentrate on even smaller measurements and make my goal that streetlight or those three trees. I don't look up the huge hill to the stoplight. That goal is too large and unreachable—but I can take one more step. I also don't look all the way home. The distance seems too far to go—but I can run to the next flower. So step by step, I complete my run. I reach my goal. With God to guide and empower, I make it through my day.

Focusing on today helps us live each day to the fullest, and that focus begins with preparation, planning, and prayer. Having done these things, we then proceed— one step at a time, one task at a time—focusing our energy on each task as it comes along throughout the day. This focus on today helps us competently scale the mountain of today as we refuse to think about the mountain range of tomorrows.

Guideline #5: Trust God to Provide

As we proceed in faith and obedience, keeping our focus on today and expecting to see God at work in our life along the way, an amazing thing happens. We find that, whatever the challenge, task, trial, crisis, or interruption, God provides for us. Whatever happens, God provides wisdom (James 1:5). Whatever happens, God provides His strength (Philippians 4:13; Deuteronomy 33:25; 2 Peter 1:3). Whatever happens, God provides what we need (Philippians 4:19). When God commands, He enables us to obey that command. Discover this wondrous truth by stepping out in trust as you walk through your day with the Lord. Not a day will go by without you experiencing His care.

Preparing, planning, praying, and proceeding enable us to focus on today because they draw us closer to God who frees us from the anxiety and worry that would keep us from loving Him with all our mind. These steps also enable us to experience God's provision for us amid the practical details of daily living. Preparing, planning, praying, and proceeding can help us experience God's provision as He helps us meet the emotional, physical, and mental challenges of each day as well.

4

Living One Day at a Time

&

Do not be anxious for tomorrow;
for tomorrow will care for itself.
Each day has enough trouble of its own.
Matthew 6:34

&

When the Persian Gulf War broke out, I had to learn to focus on today for more than having food on the table, providing clean clothes for my family, or being ready for speaking engagements. The fighting in Kuwait forced me to focus on today in my emotional life. I had to practice the five principles of preparing, planning, praying, proceeding, and then trusting God to provide when it came to the prospect of my husband going to war.

When Jim and I were first married, he joined the Army Reserves. As a registered pharmacist, he was assigned to the Medical Service Corps, where he has served since 1966. After 25 years of routine monthly meetings, we were not prepared for what happened in late 1990. In September, Operation Desert Shield began to heat up. The first signs that something big was about to happen passed without recognition. Then the initial escalation of military presence was followed by rumors that reserve units would be called up. In October, it happened: Operation Desert Shield became Operation Desert Storm, and that meant war.

I was upstairs, sitting on the edge of the bed, watching television, and holding my breath as President George Bush spoke the words we dreaded. He was authorizing the call-up of reservists. At first officials told Jim, "Oh, it's just a scare tactic. Nothing will happen." But soon actual call-ups began across the country. Still, at his unit meetings, Jim heard, "There's no way our unit is going to be called. They'll never take us." But, just in case, his unit began to prepare for the possibility. They were put on a series of practice alerts, and officers called homes to be sure they had the correct phone numbers for reaching their personnel. Next, there were emergency drills and night meetings so that the commanding officers were sure they could expedite a call-up.

One weekend in October, my husband returned from his monthly drill reporting that the leaders had stopped saying, "If we go" and were now saying, "When we go." Unit members spent the next monthly meeting packing for war. That Thanksgiving our family went away for four days together. Jim had been told he should plan to be in Saudi Arabia before Christmas. The military wanted all of its troops in place before the Christmas holiday.

Soon, all medical units on the West Coast were in Saudi Arabia except Jim's. His would be the next. . . . One hundred reservists from his unit were activated and an additional one hundred were put on alert. . . . Word came that Jim as well as the remainder of his unit were on official alert. That meant that Jim's duffel bag was packed and by the door and that he was to be within four hours of his unit at all times. Jim was issued a gas mask and trained extensively on how to use it. He was instructed to get a physical exam, update his insurance forms and his will, and be sure his family files were in order. . . .

One morning while Jim was shaving, the phone rang. He was being called up for service in the unit office in downtown Los Angeles for two weeks. All reservists spend two weeks a year on active duty, usually in the summer, but because of the war, Jim was called to fulfill his two-week obligation during the winter. His assignment was to process the soldiers leaving for the war, an assignment that was made when his superiors had noticed that Jim is a minister. They decided he would be a perfect replacement for the Family Services officer who had been sent to the Persian Gulf. Jim's job was to support the spouses and families of deployed soldiers.

Suddenly every time our phone rang at home, it was a different woman in tears. "I don't know where my husband is" came the cry. "It's been three weeks, and I haven't heard a word." Finances were another common cause for worry—"He's been gone for two months, and I haven't received his paycheck. What are we going to do without any money?"

The duties of the Family Services officer included leading support group meetings for family members left behind. At the meetings, Jim updated them on finances and available services and offered children as well as spouses help in coping with depression and anxiety. Usually a large number of people attended, and I often went along with Jim. As the people shared their worries and concerns, I joined in their tears— and I left those meetings thinking, "This is going to be me next month..."

My anguished waiting ended on March 6, 1991, when President Bush announced, "The war is over." Jim learned later that he was within one week of going overseas.

Managing Emotions

The months between October and March were an emotional roller coaster ride for me. Daily I struggled with the emotions which came with not knowing what

the future held for Jim and me. Fear, anxiety, uncertainty—I had to cope with these emotions daily. The
practical issues of life—managing schedules, housework, meals, work, and school responsibilities—are
challenge enough, but harder for me is managing emotions. For most of us, our family members are our
greatest concern. We find ourselves worrying about our
husbands and children, doing all we can to nurture our
marriage and family relationships, caring about brothers
and sisters, and agonizing over aging parents. Another
emotionally charged area is finances. Corporate layoffs,
salary cuts, the rising cost of living, growing families,
increasing expenses, the loss of retirement benefits, and
a sagging economy do indeed cause emotional stress.
What can we do with these realities that drain our emotions?

As we did for the practicalities of everyday life, we
can again turn to Matthew 6:34 for guidance in dealing
with the emotions of life. The same directives from our
Savior apply: "Do not be anxious for tomorrow; for
tomorrow will care for itself. Each day has enough
trouble of its own."

During the Persian Gulf War, I had nowhere else to
turn for help. Anxiety was pressing in from every direction. All I had was this command from Christ—and I
learned that it was all I needed because it pointed me to
Him. Jesus called me to handle my emotions one day at a
time, so I applied the same five principles—prepare,
plan, pray, proceed, and trust God's provision—to my
raging emotions.

Jim and I prepared. We cut our budget. We stopped
using our credit cards. We stopped making major pur-
chases. We wanted to have no debts other than our
mortgage. We also checked into possible jobs for me and
did some home repairs. Jim talked with the seminary
about his employment, salary, and job responsibilities.
He met with mortgage company officials to make special

arrangements for our situation and called the college our two daughters attended to check on their tuition payment policy for activated military parents.

We planned. Jim talked to our daughters at length about what might happen and about what his deployment and even his possible death would mean for them. I put my speaking engagements on hold, and, pulling together as a family, we took that four-day Thanksgiving vacation. Jim and I also pulled together as a couple. We discussed every option, every step, every phase, even down to my asking Jim, "What do you want me to do if you don't come back?" He gave me clear and specific instructions for the future.

We prayed. Like never before, Jim and I prayed. I also enlisted the help of "The Faithful Five," a group of women I have had praying friendships with for several years. I phoned each of these women and asked them to pray for me every day. I wanted them to know exactly what was going on in my life, and I called them whenever something happened—an alert, an emergency drill, any news from the Army.

In addition to my praying, I fasted. God alone could keep my husband from going to war. There was nothing I could do, and there was nothing Jim could do. There was no human way out. So, I began to fast on December 4. I decided to break my fast each day at sundown, a format which followed the Jewish model and which happened to correspond to the 5 P.M. close of all Army offices. No phone calls commanding my husband to report to duty in Desert Storm would come after five o'clock. On that first day, I also decided that I would fast until I knew Jim was not going to the Persian Gulf or, if he did go, until he came back—or died. That was my covenant with God.

During this time of fasting, God alone knew of the four trials, equal in magnitude to the Persian Gulf War, that I would later face, trials involving the health of one daughter, cancer biopsies for me, a critical financial crisis, and an extremely difficult relationship with another person. In fact, God seemed to use this war to force me into a position of total dependence on Him so that I would better handle those other four situations. In the end, prayer and fasting availed as much for those four situations as for the 63rd Army Command.

We proceeded. Besides calling us to prepare and plan, Jesus tells us in Matthew 6:34 how to proceed—"Do not be anxious for tomorrow." As I went about my daily life, I was to let this verse set boundaries for my thoughts. God was telling me not to speculate on my future. He wasn't asking me to handle my entire life all at once. He was wisely telling me to limit my thoughts to today, to what was real now. My "what if" imaginings about the future—as we saw in the first two chapters—were not real, and therefore I didn't need to deal with them. But today was real, and I had to deal with it. With God's strength and grace, I would be able to function today. I wouldn't be able to if I were anxious about tomorrow. So I chose to draw near to the God who loves me and promises to care for me and to love Him with all my mind by attempting to keep my thoughts within His prescribed boundary of today.

Choosing to love God with my mind also helped limit my emotions because thoughts generate emotions. Without God's command to limit my thinking, I don't think I could have emotionally handled all that God asked me to during the Persian Gulf War and after. But, through Matthew 6:34, God was telling me not to feel the emotions that would come in the yet-unrevealed future. "Do not be anxious" spoke directly to my heart. I let today be the boundary for my fears and emotions. I proceeded with each day as it came, knowing that God was with me.

Every day, however, seemed like an entire lifetime. Emotionally, physically, and spiritually, I was strained to the limit. Each time the phone rang during these long months, it was bad news. It was Jim's unit, or a distraught spouse, or another doctor, or more test results, or an order for another biopsy. In addition, I was living with my husband as if each day was our last and, at the same time, trying to be sensitive to our children's worries, fears, and needs.

Moments of peace came only as I followed the wisdom of Matthew 6:34. I fought to keep my thoughts and feelings focused to one day at a time, but I often found myself being a lot like Charlie Brown who glumly reports in one "Peanuts" cartoon, "I used to try to take each day as it came, but my philosophy has changed. I'm down to half a day at a time!"

I also found great guidance and wisdom from the writings of missionary Elisabeth Elliot. Sometimes, for instance, I would think I was silly to feel so much anxiety about my husband's potential service in a war. No, he didn't go overseas and, no, he didn't die. But I only knew that after the fact, so for many months, fear was a daily reality for me. Elisabeth Elliot helped me understand the intensity of my emotions with her observation that "People who have themselves experienced both grief and fear know how alike those two things are. . . . They are equally disabling, distracting and destructive."[1]

Elisabeth Elliot does indeed know fear and grief. When she was serving in the jungles of Ecuador, she and the other missionary wives received word that two bodies had been found at the location where their husbands had gone. What did she think? How did she feel? First, she focused her mind on God and the truth in His Word. "It was the first I knew that anything was amiss," she recalls. "A verse God had impressed on my mind when I first arrived in Ecuador came back suddenly and sharply: 'When thou passest through the waters, I will be with thee, and through the rivers, they shall not overflow thee. . . .'"[2] Armed with this promise of God's presence, she prayed and proceeded to go about her duties. "I went upstairs to continue teaching the Indian girls' literacy class, praying silently, 'Lord, let not the waters overflow.'"[3]

Jim Elliot was one of the men who was killed, and the way his wife faced this crisis helped me face mine. I wanted to quit. I felt angry, and I wanted to fall down in a heap and cry, focus on myself, and forget about everyone else and their needs. But I knew that is not how God would have His people face a crisis. I had to proceed with my duties and responsibilities. I had to go on living life. As I did so, I experienced the truth of something else Elisabeth Elliot has written: "At such times I have been wonderfully calmed and strengthened by doing some simple duty . . . like a bed to be made or a kitchen floor to be washed. . . . Sometimes it takes everything you have to get up and do it, but it is surprising how strength comes."[4]

In times of emotional stress, strength does come from routine and responsibility. That is another reason why it is important that we have a plan for the day. Life must go on, and we must function. Our families need care, and our homes must be kept in order. Doing tasks towards these ends keeps us from being immobilized by depression and fear. As Elisabeth Elliot points out, "There is wonderful therapy in getting up and doing something. While you are doing, time passes quickly. Time itself will in some measure heal. . . . And in the doing of whatever comes next, we are shown what to do after that."[5]

And where had Mrs. Elliot, a model of Christian maturity for me, learned how to function when catastrophe struck? Jesus Christ had shown her the way. "Our Lord did not halt all activity to brood over what was to come," she writes. "He was not incapacitated by the fear of suffering, though he well knew that fear. To the question, 'What shall I do?' (so often, for us, the cry of despair) he simply answered, 'This,' and did what lay in his path to do at the moment, trusting himself completely into the hands of his Father. This is how he endured the cross."[6]

For nine months of waiting, praying, and fasting—for the war, my daughter's health, my biopsies, our finances, and a painful relationship—I tried to follow Jesus' example and the principles of Matthew 6:34. For nine months, I tried to take one day at a time. Nine months is 270 days of living one day at a time, 270 days of not being anxious about tomorrow, 270 days of handling the trouble of each day as it came, 270 days of not allowing myself to look ahead or feel in advance the worries of 269 tomorrows. I had to prepare, plan, and pray. I also had to proceed. I had to live each day as it came, one day at a time. I had to forego my selfish desires to withdraw and to quit.

And, as I lived one day at a time, *I saw God provide* for me each day. The fact that I am writing about this experience three years later is a witness to God's provision for me—to His presence with me and to His work in my life—as I proceeded one day at a time. The final entry in my journal from that time of my life remains a real touchstone for me: "God, You are so good in Your dealings with me and with my family! Thank You for arranging my life so that I need You so greatly. Thank You for the intimate closeness of my walk with You these past months. Thank You for the humility I feel, the lowliness, the dependency, the brokenness, the cleanness. Thank You for opening the floodgates of my heart for so many others—and at the time of my greatest need! Because You have so adequately met my needs, I can give to others in need. I have needed You and I have sought You, and You have been there in new ways. I know that I have grown in faith. It was tested daily, and I now know You better."

When I look back on that challenging time, I am well aware of all that I learned about God. Did He enable me to deal with the circumstances and the stress? Was His grace sufficient? Did spiritual growth occur in my life? Am I a stronger Christian today because of that experience? Did I move toward spiritual maturity? Do I know more about my God today? Do I know more about waiting, suffering, trusting, and persevering? Am I stronger in my faith? Can I better relate to people's pain? Can I be a more effective minister and servant now? Yes—and a thousand more yeses! My faith was tested daily, and the only way to pass those tests was, by God's grace, one day at a time.

Managing Affliction

Like emotional stress, physical suffering calls us to follow the principles of Matthew 6:34 and focus on one day at a time. I know women who suffer from incurable diseases, who deal with physical limitations every waking moment, who have nursed husbands or parents dying from cancer, who have children confined to wheelchairs, and who have died from breast cancer. How do they live when physical suffering is a part of their daily reality?

Edith Schaeffer, the wife of theologian and writer Dr. Francis Schaeffer and co-founder with him of the Swiss retreat L'Abri, knows about living with a loved one's physical suffering. When medical tests done here in the United States revealed that Dr. Schaeffer had cancer, he told his wife those "awful words that turned our world upside down."[7]

One thing Edith did after her world was turned upside down was find a biblical perspective on the circumstances she faced. She needed "basic truth and God's Word [to] take the center of thoughts and feelings."[8] She wrote, "We are always living on the edge of disaster, change, shock, or attack. Peace, and the affluence to enjoy that peace, are always a false separation from the reality of the raging battle. . . . Not only is our understanding blurred of what the Fall actually consists of, but our understanding of the absolute *marvel* of what God has done for us in making victory certain and complete is dimmed!"[9] Edith knew Scripture's teaching that we will suffer in this world, and she recognized that peace and good times are fleeting on this earth. She also saw confirmed in the Bible the sterility of a life without suffering as well as God's provision for certain victory in suffering.

So, armed with spiritual truth, Edith Schaeffer *prepared* for their time of physical trial. She remembers, "I felt [it] imperative . . . to make a home for Fran as soon as possible, if he were to stay here for treatment—whether he had six weeks or six months to live! . . . Why a 'home'? I would answer that home is important to a person to help him or her get well, as well as being important for family times together if someone is dying. In either case, beauty and familiar surroundings have an effect on the physical, psychological, and even spiritual state."[10]

Edith Schaeffer also *planned*. The diagnosis of cancer gave the family some waiting time, and Mrs. Schaeffer learned that " 'marking time' is never the way to wait. . . . [C]reative ideas need to begin to take place in one's imagination. . . . Even in times of shock, waiting can be something more than sitting in abject fear."[11] Planning was one of the ways Mrs. Schaeffer used her waiting time: "Doing interior decorating inside your head while in a hospital or clinic waiting room is a positive creative activity—as well as a way of planning for demonstrating your love and concern for the person you love."[12]

During this waiting time, Mrs. Schaeffer also *prayed*. Every single day, throughout each stage of the cancer, and before, during, and after every doctor's report, Edith Schaeffer prayed. And what did she pray? "Don't let any one of us stop trusting you now, Lord. Please may our love be real for you—solid oak, not a thin veneer. This is the time that counts for your glory; don't let us blow it.... Please, Father, give us victory...."[13] She also asked God to give her husband "time and strength to show forth God's strength and power to the next generation."[14]

Having prepared, planned, and prayed, Mrs. Schaeffer *proceeded*. With three days of cleaning, painting, and assembling an odd assortment of furnishings, she made a home for her beloved husband. She provided opportunities for the family to be together. She thoroughly researched cancer, chemotherapy, vitamins, and diet and proceeded with the daily challenges of caring for a cancer patient. Mrs. Schaeffer writes, "'One-day-at-a-time' became an important measure to be constantly met.... When you are supposed to die in a short period of time, the dates are more appreciated; the 'and thens' take on a bit of sparkle!"[15]

As Edith Schaeffer proceeded, *Dr. Schaeffer proceeded as well*. Despite his suffering, he continued to minister. He spoke to large gatherings of doctors and local residents and answered their questions about God, life, and death. He "went on in the midst of cancer, trusting the Lord, and continuing to care about other people... [realizing] there is more to life than being 'comfortable' and 'happy'; there is growth going on...."[16]

God provided for them as Dr. and Mrs. Schaeffer proceeded. Even when Dr. Schaeffer felt so dizzy he thought he couldn't speak, Mrs. Schaeffer notes, "Strength came in a sufficient quantity.... Just enough energy 'was given' to carry on each time. It [wasn't] that Fran felt great. Rather he felt he could ask for the Lord's strength in measure for the needs and that it wasn't time to 'give up' when he could be a help."[17]

During the five years that her husband suffered, Edith Schaeffer focused on today. She took one day at a time and relied on God to be with her. Day to day and moment to moment, she prepared, planned, prayed, and proceeded with her duties and responsibilities. And day to day and moment to moment, she experienced God's provision for her. She did not give up or quit. She dealt with her emotions when they came, but she never ceased to be a selfless woman, wife, and mother. "Looking back on it," she says, "I don't think I'd do anything differently."[18] Even as she faced enormous emotional and physical challenges, Mrs. Schaeffer had lived out of God's grace each and every day, one day at a time.

Managing Today

So where does today find you? What are the circumstances of your life? Are your emotions stretched to the limit? Is physical affliction taxing you or a loved one? What fires are purifying your faith? Whatever our situation, God calls us to live one day at a time. Again, quoting our Savior, we are not to "be anxious for tomorrow; for tomorrow will care for itself. Each day has enough trouble of its own" (Matthew 6:34).

Whether your particular challenge is physical, emotional, mental, or a combination, the strategy of preparing, planning, praying, and proceeding will help you manage life's demands—one day at a time. Then, as you proceed through each day, you will experience God's love in very personal ways as you discover His complete provision. You will witness a daily miracle as you find God meeting you in the circumstances of your life and giving you the strength you need when you need it.

God does indeed enable us to live according to His instruction to focus on today. With Him, you and I can successfully climb the mountain of today, leaving the mountain range of tomorrows to tomorrow. And the peace that comes with knowing that we are following God's guidance day by day, moment by moment, frees us to better love God with all our mind.

5

Remembering to Forget

———— 🙟 ————

Forgetting what lies behind . . .
Philippians 3:13

———— 🙟 ————

Although I've never attended one of my high-school reunions, I've heard a great deal about those events. My friends have told me about classmates who still look the way they always did and others whose personality hasn't changed at all. They also report that others are larger and balder and therefore unrecognizable. Sadly, some who enjoyed success during their high-school years have gone the way of alcoholism, divorce, and other tragedies.

The past. It makes us who we are. It teaches us lessons about God, about life, and about ourselves. We are to learn from what lies behind, but then we are to take those lessons and move ahead. That is what the apostle Paul talks about in Philippians 3:13-14, another one of my breakthrough passages. After exalting Jesus Christ and exhorting us to be like Him in Philippians 2, Paul now tells us in Philippians 3 how to pursue Christlikeness. Acknowledging that he himself has not yet arrived, Paul shares three actions that help him continue his progress toward Christlikeness and spiritual maturity: "*Forgetting* what lies behind and *reaching forward* to what lies ahead, I *press on* toward the goal for the prize of the upward call of God in Christ Jesus" (emphasis mine). We'll look at these steps in the next three chapters.

The first step toward living a life that pleases Christ, a life that culminates in eternal glory with our Lord, is forgetting what lies behind. The past, however, isn't always easy to forget. Whether it's success we haven't experienced since or some failure we haven't quite let go of, the past can have quite a hold on our mind and our heart. I know because thinking too much about past injuries, insults, and sorrows once made sadness, melancholy, and weeping part of my every day. Dwelling on the past—on the kind of disappointments, struggles, and failures we all experience—made me tired and depressed and quickly became a breeding ground for bitterness. The more I thought about what had happened to me—things like a cruel remark remembered from high school, rejection from a boyfriend, being passed over after that first job interview, or the death of Jim's father—the deeper I sank into darkness and despair. And looking at the past offered me nothing in the way of hope or light or answers.

The apostle Paul's words in Philippians 3:13-14, however, gave me the guidance I needed to open myself to God's grace and begin to overcome the daily negative lifestyle which grew out of my unhealthy dwelling on the past. Paul is our example as he forgets, reaches forward, and presses on. Let's look now at the first step Paul takes as he pursues Christlikeness—forgetting what lies behind.

Forgetting the Past

As we begin looking at Paul's example of forgetting the past, let me again say that the past is important: It shapes us, it teaches us, and it reminds us of God's faithfulness. Our spiritual growth, however, can be blocked by inordinate attention to the past. Dwelling on the past can induce "a slackening of pace" in our Christian walk.[1] It is too easy to look backward and never move forward or, as one commentator puts it, "looking back is sure to end in going back."[2] Christian growth—the process of moving forward—"requires . . . looking to the future rather than to the past."[3] One commentator writes, "The Christian's onward progress is hindered should he dwell on the past full of failures and sins, full of heartaches and discouragements, full of disappointments and thwarted hopes and plans. As long as a Christian has made things right with God and man, he should completely forget the past."[4]

Paul's language in Philippians 3 is indeed as strong as the commentary suggests. Another biblical scholar writes, "When Paul says that he forgets what lies behind, he refers to a type of forgetting which is no mere, passive oblivion. It is active obliteration, so that when any thought of . . . the past would occur to Paul, he immediately banished it from his mind. . . . It is a constant, deliberate discarding of any thought of [the] past. . . ."[5] Another commentator explains, "Forgetting is stronger in the Greek, [meaning] 'completely forgetting'" and translates Paul's words, "I in fact am forgetting completely the things that are behind."[6]

Christians of old took Paul's advice to forget what lies behind more seriously than we do today. F. B. Meyer, writing in his celebrated devotional commentary at the turn of the century, addressed "The Duty of Forgetting," and called for "No morbid dwelling on the Sinful Past." He appealed to his readers to "learn to forget . . . and do not dwell upon past sin. . . . There may be things in our past of which we are ashamed, which might haunt us, which might cut the sinews of our strength. But if we have handed them over to God in confession and faith, He has put them away and forgotten them. Forget them, and . . . the sin which has vitiated and blackened your record, [and] reach forward to realise the beauty of Jesus."[7]

Forgetting what lies behind, however, is not always easy, and note that the word "forgetting" is in the present tense. Forgetting is not an act done once and for all. Instead, like Paul, we must keep on forgetting those things in the past which hold us back. Paul doesn't want to rest on his past accomplishments, and neither should we. Paul doesn't want his past mistakes to keep him from moving on, and neither should we. Again and again, I have told myself, "No, Liz, that is past. That is over. That is no longer real. So don't dwell on it. Don't let it hold you back. Forget that which would keep you from moving forward in faith and in your spiritual growth." I look to the past only to remember God's role in the problems and pain of yesterday—His gracious provision for me, His presence, His faithfulness, and His compassion.

Looking to the past for lessons God has taught us and forgetting those elements of the past which would stymie our progress forward may sound like a tricky balance to maintain. What does the apostle Paul teach us about forgetting those elements of the past which would block our Christian growth and our progress toward Christlikeness?

Forgetting the Bad

One thing we do well to forget is the bad we did before we became Christians. Before he came to know Jesus as Lord and Savior, Paul was Saul, the persecutor of Christians, whom one scholar called "the guiding spirit of evil"[8] and another described as acting with "brutal cruelty...[as] a wild animal savaging a body."[9] The Bible tells of Paul "ravaging the church, entering house after house; and dragging off men and women...[and putting] them in prison" (Acts 8:3). It is also quite possible that, rather than merely witnessing the stoning of

Stephen, Paul was involved in the sentencing and gave his wholehearted approval to the murder (Acts 7:58; 8:1). On his way to Damascus, with letters from the high priest authorizing him to bind and bring Christian men and women to Jerusalem for trial (Acts 9:1-2), Paul met Jesus Christ. Only this encounter with Christ kept Paul's hands from being bloodied even further.

While you and I may not have committed murder, many of us did things before we knew Christ which we must forget if we are to grow as Christians. What can you and I do when those past sins come to mind? First, we need to remind ourselves of the truth of 2 Corinthians 5:17—"If any man is in Christ, he is a new creature; the old things passed away; behold, new things have come." If you are a Christian, you are a new creature. You have "been created all over again."[10] Old things, including the sin you committed before coming to know Jesus, have passed away and are gone forever. All that you were and all that you did as a non-Christian are gone forever, removed "as far as the east is from the west" (Psalm 103:12). As Corrie Ten Boom loved to say, "When we confess our sins, God casts them into the deepest ocean, gone forever. And even though I cannot find a Scripture for it, I believe God then places a sign out there that says, NO FISHING ALLOWED."[11]

God's love for you accomplished the forgiveness of your sin, your cleansing, your new birth, and your fresh start. Consequences of your actions may remain, but the sin itself is forgiven. You are covered and cleansed by Christ's precious blood. You can therefore go on without shame and without being held back, and you can show your love for God by refusing to dwell on what He has removed. When your past sin comes to mind, acknowledge God's forgiveness, thank Him, and move on.

Besides letting go of those sins committed before naming Jesus as Lord and Savior, Paul—and you and I—need to let go of the sins we have committed and the bad things that have happened to us since we became Christians. The apostle Paul suffered great things for the sake of Christ (Acts 9:16). He experienced beatings, betrayal, hunger, and thirst because of his faith in Jesus Christ (see 2 Corinthians 11:23-27). God also allowed Satan to afflict Paul with "a thorn in the flesh" (2 Corinthians 12:7). Dwelling on these things and asking why they happened would have indeed blocked Paul's growth in the Lord. He needed to forget them, in the way we have defined the term, and move on.

Undoubtedly, certain events in life—acts done to us or by us, acts which have consequences we must deal with as innocent victims, and acts we have witnessed— also need to be forgotten if we are to move on and grow in the Lord. Several years ago, for instance, my daughter Katherine witnessed a tiny boy being physically abused by his father. Her employer wrote down the man's license plate number and reported him to the police, but what was Katherine to do with her memory of the abuse, the sounds she had heard, and the anxiety she had felt? When she told Jim and me about the incident, we agonized with her and we prayed—for Katherine, for the man, for the boy, and for the police. We also prayed for her to begin the process of forgetting. We encouraged her to, through prayer, leave the situation in God's capable hands and then obliterate any thought of what she witnessed. She had to go on.

When Laurie called me about her niece Anna, I knew she also needed to let go of the past and move on. Anna had had an extremely abusive childhood and her nightmares had begun again. As Laurie and I talked about how she might help her niece, I mentioned, "And be sure she isn't watching too much news." Laurie said, "That's it, Liz! When I was at her home, we watched the news together, and now I remember what was on the news. No wonder the nightmares started up again." The news story had brought back the past for Anna when she was trying to move on from it.

God wants Katherine, Anna, and you and me to move on from the suffering of the past. He doesn't want the circumstances and situations of life to weigh us down with guilt, result in bitterness, or cause us to question Him and His goodness. Whatever suffering you've experienced (from unexplainable losses to someone's thoughtless comment) and whenever it happened (twenty years or two minutes ago), God's remedy is the same: Forget what lies behind. Let it lie behind you. Keep it in the past. Don't let the pain or the questions keep you down. Acknowledge that God's ways are not our ways (Isaiah 55:8), that innocents suffer when people sin, that we live in a fallen world—and go on with life. In other words, remember to forget!

Forgetting the Good

Although it may surprise you, Paul needed to forget the good as well as the bad of his past if he were to serve the Lord effectively. Before he became a Christian, he enjoyed a multitude of privileges as a Roman citizen and student of Gamaliel, the great teacher of the law. Paul's impeccable Jewish pedigree meant an enviable position in society (Philippians 3:5-6). Paul, however, chose to forget his status and the privileges of his position, regarding them as a hindrance to running the race for Christ. Answering God's call on his life, Paul served God and His eternal truth and valued that far more than the fleeting status and privilege the world offered him.

In more recent times, C. T. Studd, like Paul, forgot the good that he had enjoyed before becoming a Christian. Extremely wealthy and Cambridge-educated, Studd was one of the seven men from that college who began the world missions movement in the nineteenth century.

As these men left for China, a news correspondent described them as "standing side by side renouncing the careers in which they had already gained no small distinction, putting aside the splendid prizes of earthly ambition, taking leave of the social circles in which they shone with no mean brilliance, and plunging into that warfare whose splendours are seen only by faith, and whose rewards seem so shadowy to the unopened vision of ordinary men."[12]

Later, before leaving on his second trip to China, C. T. Studd "invested in the Bank of Heaven by giving away all of his inheritance" except for 3,400 British pounds which he presented to his bride before their wedding. She, too, knew about forgetting what lies behind. She asked, "Now, Charlie, what did the Lord tell the rich young man to do?" When C. T. answered, "Sell all," she said, "Well, then, we will start clear with the Lord at our wedding." She anonymously gave the 3,400 pounds to General Booth of the Salvation Army.[13]

God made the world and declared it good, but even the good—even God's blessings—can keep us from serving the Lord with all of our energy, all of our heart, and all of our self. The apostle Paul and missionary C. T. Studd moved on from the good, which the world offered and which they knew before becoming Christians, to serve the better which their God had for them.

Paul also had to move on from the good which he experienced after becoming a follower of Jesus Christ. A brilliant orator, Paul had led great numbers of people to salvation. He worked many miracles and healings, and Christ spoke to him three times. Paul saw visions, received revelations, was "caught up to the third heaven . . . into Paradise, and heard inexpressible words" (2 Corinthians 12:2,4). God used Paul mightily to minister to early believers, and today his writings comprise thirteen books of the New Testament. Even accomplishments like these, however, when dwelled on too long, can keep us from reaching forward in our journey toward Christlike-ness. We cannot make progress when we are resting on our laurels, so we must forget the good. I saw this truth sadly illustrated several years ago.

The couple arrived at our church fresh from serving in a fine Christian organization for ten years. They seemed to have been everywhere and done everything for Christ. As a new Christian, I saw what they had and, for a while, I wanted it.

But during the next ten years of their life, I saw them float along on the merits of their former service. They regularly reminded us of their ten-year term with that worthy organization, but they did nothing in the present. Drawing on their past, this couple reminded me of the man at a Hollywood party who, feeling snubbed, went from guest to guest saying, "But you don't know who I was!"

It's far too easy for us Christians to say, like the man at the party, "But you don't know who I was . . . back on the East Coast, or in my old church, or where I grew up, or when I was on the mission field, or when I served with this organization. You don't know who I was!" We are like the star in the sky which, as Dr. John MacArthur explains, died but which we could see for thirty more years. "Its brilliance," he said, "was from the past, but it was dead in the present." God doesn't want His people to be like that star, so through Paul, He says, "Forget 'who you was!' What are you doing *now*?"

God wants us to forget our achievements, our accomplishments, and our brilliance so that we will keep achieving and accomplishing for Him in the present. Stopping to remember the good ol' days can too easily become dwelling on them and becoming immobile in our work for the Lord. Good things in the past can keep us from looking and moving forward, so Paul says, "Forget what lies behind." Whether they happened twenty years ago or yesterday, the wonderful things you have accomplished or experienced are to be forgotten. These things are dead in the present—although we don't always realize that fact.

Writing of some time he spent with a group of Christian leaders, pastor Chuck Swindoll reports, "While everyone else much preferred to be on a first-name basis (rather than Reverend or Mister) one man demanded: 'Call ME doctor.'" Chuck's advice to "Dr. Hotshot" was "Get a good education—but get over it. Dig in and pay the price for solid, challenging years in school, and apply your education with all your ability, but PLEASE spare others from the tiring reminders of how honored they should feel in your presence. Reach the maximum of your potential—but DON'T TALK ABOUT IT." He then dared all his fellow pastors to remove all the diplomas from the walls in their offices and any object that promoted them and their achievements.[14] Such signs of past achievement mean nothing next to what we are doing for God today.

Writing about Paul's example to us of the value of forgetting the past, one commentator notes that "the memory of past successes and attainments may detain us from more splendid triumphs. . . . [Paul did] not please himself by dwelling on . . . what he had accomplished. No; his thought was what was yet to be accomplished. What was there yet possible to him of Christian experience, of Christian usefulness?"[15] He refused to succumb to self-satisfaction. With his gaze focused on the future, Paul knew that "the Christian must forget all that he has done and remember only what he still has to do."[16] We are to thank God for the good of the past and the good He has enabled us to do for Him. Then we are to move on and serve God in the present.

Three Steps for Forgetting

Forgetting the past—holding lightly the good God

has blessed us with and used us to accomplish and not questioning the unexplainable bad that has come our way—is not easy to do. The following three steps, however, may help you let go of whatever God would have you forget of the past so that you are free to serve Him in the present.

First, find the gold. Whatever has happened to you in the past and whatever is happening in your life now, look for the hidden blessing, the lesson to be learned, or the character trait being forged. Trust that, since God has allowed these experiences, somewhere there is gold for you and remember that gold isn't always easily seen or readily accessible. After all, during the Gold Rush, the miners dipped their pans in the filth on the bottom of a stream and drew up a plate of silt, gravel, and stones. Patiently and carefully, they sifted through the dirt, eliminating all that was without value and hoping to find gold shining purely and brilliantly through the refuse they dredged from the riverbed. Many did indeed make their fortunes but not without a lot of work. And it may take some work on our part to find the good God is working in the bad of our life.

I encourage you to take some time to think back on the bad things of your life. Without dwelling on them, look for some positive despite the negative. Look for where our merciful and loving God is working redemption in the situations. The good you find may be a lesson learned, deeper knowledge of God, or greater understanding for further service to Him and His people (2 Corinthians 1:4). Find the good and let go of the rest. Take the good with you and move on.

Once you find the gold, you will need to find forgiveness for the bad that resulted from your sin. As we saw in chapter one, "If we confess our sins, [God] is faithful and righteous to forgive us our sins and to cleanse us from all unrighteousness" (1 John 1:9). The truth is that you are forgiven, and this truth cost Christ His life. Let the truth of God's gracious forgiveness help you let go of the past. After all, as my pastor asks, "Why should you remember what God has forgotten?" Know that you are forgiven.

Finally, having found the gold and God's forgiveness, forgive those who have hurt you. Jesus models such forgiveness for us as, hanging on the cross, He prays, "Father, forgive them; for they do not know what they are doing" (Luke 23:34). When we fail to follow Christ's example—when we fail to forgive others—we sentence ourselves to a life of bitterness. We also stop growing in our faith, and we compromise our service and witness for Jesus. When, by God's grace, we are able to extend forgiveness to those who have hurt us, we can be used mightily by God. Helen Roseveare, a missionary doctor who was brutally raped while serving in The Congo, forgave those who wronged her and returned to the same location for twenty more years of missionary service.[17] When Elisabeth Elliot forgave the men who savagely killed her missionary husband, she was able to return and continue her ministry of the gospel of forgiveness.[18] And Corrie Ten Boom struggled greatly to forgive the German soldier who had been cruelest to her sister and herself while they were prisoners at Ravensbruck during World War II. Had she not been able to forgive that guard, Corrie Ten Boom could have had no ministry to anyone.[19] Dr. Helen Roseveare, Elisabeth Elliot, and Corrie Ten Boom all found freedom from the past and freedom to serve when they extended forgiveness to those who had hurt them deeply—and you and I can, too.

Forgetting what lies behind is key to finding freedom from a past which would hold back our Christian growth. Forgetting what lies behind is also the first step the apostle Paul took as he ran the race and lived his life for Jesus Christ. What do you need to let go of from the past? Are you resting on the laurels of past achievements for the Lord? What major accomplishment may be hindering your effort to run the Christian race? Thank God for using you as He has, and then ask Him to show you where He would have you move forward for Him.

Perhaps you are being held to the past by a source of deep pain or an experience which makes it hard to understand God's role in the universe. Ask God to shine His light in your darkness (Psalm 112:4) and help you find the gold of His redemptive work in your life. Where appropriate, admit any wrong acts or thoughts and ask God's forgiveness and, also where appropriate, ask God's help in forgiving others.

With the gold gleaned from the past and forgiveness both extended and received, you can now reach forward and tackle the challenges of the present with all your energy. That is the next step Paul identifies for us as we continue to experience God's freeing and empowering love, an experience which enables us to love Him with all our mind.

6

Going On and
On and On

———— ❧ ————

Reaching forward to what lies ahead . . .
Philippians 3:13

———— ❧ ————

The missionary wanted to teach the people Philippians 3:13-14, where, as we have seen, the apostle Paul writes, "Brethren, I do not regard myself as having laid hold of [spiritual maturity or Christlike perfection] yet; but one thing I do: forgetting what lies behind and reaching forward to what lies ahead, I press on toward the goal for the prize of the upward call of God in Christ Jesus." Several days after the lesson, one of his students approached the missionary with this poem on the meaning of Paul's words:

> Go on, go on, go on, go on,
> Go on, go on, go on.
> Go on, go on, go on, go on,
> Go on, go on, go on!

And there were seven more identical stanzas to his poem! This man definitely understood Paul's message!

Paul is forgetting the elements of the past, both good and bad, which would hold back his spiritual growth, and he is determined to reach forward and move ahead. Like Paul, when we choose to forget the elements of the past which would keep us stuck there, when we leave the good and the bad of the past in God's omnipotent and redemptive hands, we make a 180° turn. No longer do we look at the past. Instead we look to what is ahead. Our no to the past—to what is behind—is also a yes to the present and what is at hand, and this focus on the present is important.

A Focused Woman

What characterizes a focused woman? What sets her apart from other women? First, a focused woman knows where she is going. She has a sense of God's call on her life, and that call gives her direction each step of the way and makes it easier for her to make decisions. With her sights set on these God-given goals, she is able to say no to the trivial. She chooses from among her options that which moves her toward her life goals.

This focus for her life also gives her greater energy for reaching that goal. She doesn't waste energy wondering what to do or wandering aimlessly from option to option. Knowing exactly what she wants to do and needs to do, she pours her energy into those things. Her knowing what to do and her knowing that God will enable her to serve Him where He has placed her gives her confidence as well as energy. She knows where she is headed and why, and she makes all that she does count for her Lord. It's this kind of focus which Paul calls us to in Philippians 3:13-14. Hear what he has to say about this focus.

A Runner's Focus

When Paul talks about "reaching forward to what lies ahead," the context of his words suggests a runner racing toward the finish line. His body bent forward, Paul fixes his eyes on his goal. Moving along the path he has set for himself, the path God has laid out for him, he leans forward as his feet carry him toward the finish. All of his energy—mental, emotional, and physical—is committed to the race he is running.

And this image is quite a contrast to the paintings of an Edwardian lady featured on some note cards I saw in a bookstore one day. With a dreamy half-smile, she lounges on a pillowed window seat. With one hand, she holds the book she is reading. With the other, she strokes the cat curled up in her lap. A gentle breeze has lifted the gauze curtains to reveal a splendid day outside. Her days of simple leisure hardly reflect the way Christ means for us to live our lives. Instead, like Paul, we are to run a race toward the goal of Christlike maturity. Besides keeping our standards high, that prize gives us reason to go on and on and on.

Like me, you may daydream about days of leisure. But, perhaps like me, you also realize that life is a race and, by God's grace, are doing your best to run it for and with Him. To stay on course, I ask myself the following questions from time to time, and these questions may help you: Am I focusing my efforts toward the prize that awaits at the end or am I too content watching other people's efforts? Am I training regularly and, by working out in the daily disciplines of the Christian life, receiving God's grace and His strength for the race? Am I properly fueling my body with sleep, nutrition, and exercise for maximum results?

Running the race—living for Christ and growing into His image—requires focus and discipline. Rest and relaxation are important as we respond to God's call on our life, but we aren't to let the desire to rest, relax, and reward ourselves interfere with our efforts for His kingdom. As Paul's words suggest, having a runner's focus can improve our race toward Christlike perfection.

Focus On the Present

Paul knows that a runner who looks backward will lose the race. As we saw in chapter 5, Paul has chosen not to allow his past failures and accomplishments to interfere with his present efforts for his Lord. That same decision to forget the past enables you and me to grow spiritually. Leaving in God's hands the elements of the past—which would hold us back and drain us of energy and emotion—is an important first step in the race toward Christlikeness, as one woman shared with me after she heard this lesson on forgetting what lies behind. She wrote, "This verse is for anyone who has ever made a mistake. What a splendid wave of comfort washes over me to realize the freedom to not look back over my past failures." Forgetting the past does indeed free us from self-flagellation and regret so that we can better receive God's love for us and love Him in return.

Recognizing God's Purpose for Us

Our runner's focus on the present comes when we clearly understand the purpose of our life, and I discovered God's purpose for me—His call on my life—in a very special way when a woman handed me a small, flat package, wrapped in muted pastels. The card read, "Thank you for your class on prayer," and the package contained a leather-bound, silver-edged book that greatly broadened my prayer life.

In *Drawing Near* (now published under the title *Scripture Talks with God*), authors Max Anders and Kenneth Boa set forth a monthly pattern for devotional prayer based on topical Scriptures. The entry on Day 31, the end of the first month, contains four questions about our identity in Christ.[1] Puzzled, I paused long enough to scratch my head and then went on. This happened each time I reached Day 31 until one month I reluctantly tackled the questions—Who am I? Where did I come from? Why am I here? and Where am I going?

The book in general changed my prayers, but an-swering these four questions changed my life. Before I answered those questions, I was greatly influenced by other people's ideas about what I should do with my life and what my Christian faith should look like. A "move-ment" follower and a "program" participant, I had al-lowed other people to determine my purpose. But these four questions helped me recognize the purpose of my life and gave me life goals on which to focus. Today I know who I am, where I came from, why I am here, where I am going. I am a Christian woman, wife, and mother; I was "in [Christ] before the foundation of the world" (Ephesians 1:4); I am here to give my life in service to God and His people; and, by the grace of God rather than my own efforts, I am going to heaven.

I encourage you to take a few minutes to answer these four questions for yourself. They will help you grasp God's great purpose for your life and give you a sense of direction as you set your goals and plan your activities. Like me, you may be awed by the realization that God has a specific purpose for you. For me, that realization has given me a better sense of mission (I am definitely more focused as a result of glimpsing God's purpose for my life); a clearer understanding of my job assignment (I am to spend myself and be spent in service to Christ and His people); and an urgency as I go about my tasks (knowing that my time on earth is limited, I am frightfully aware of time wasted and time passing). I want to use my time and my energy to achieve God's purposes and, along the way, find rest and refreshment in Him. After all, it is He who ultimately makes things happen for the kingdom. I am just thankful that He has chosen to use me in the process!

The apostle Paul was certainly used by God as he re-sponded to the God-given purpose and driving force of his life: "I press on in order that I may lay hold of that for which also I was laid hold of by Christ Jesus" (Philippians 3:12). As commentator William Barclay puts it, Paul "is trying to grasp that for which he has been grasped by Christ. . . . Paul felt that when Christ stopped him on the Damascus Road, He had a vision and a purpose for Paul; and Paul felt that all his life he was bound to press on, lest he fail Jesus and frustrate His dream. . . . Every [person] is grasped by Christ for some purpose; and, therefore, every [person] should all his life press on so that he may grasp that purpose for which Christ grasped him."[2]

We have focus for our life when we have recognized God's purpose for our life and when we, as Oswald Chambers has pointed out, center our entire being in God.[3] We are not to get tripped up or stalled by the past. Instead, we are to reach forward for that for which we have been grasped by Christ.

The Pursuit of Excellence

Once we recognize God's purpose for our life, we keep our focus sharp by pursuing excellence as we serve Him even when circumstances are difficult and painful. In Genesis 37–50, for example, Joseph forgets the past, forgives those who sinned against him, and focuses forward, modeling for us the pursuit of excellence each step of the difficult way.

Sold into slavery in Egypt by envious brothers, Joseph chooses to serve God by doing the best he can, whatever the circumstances of his life. He chooses to forget (in the sense of moving on from) his past in Israel, and he goes on to be the best slave in Egypt and, when the captain of the Pharaoh's guard bought him, the best manager of Potiphar's household—until he is unjustly imprisoned. . . . In prison, Joseph chooses to forget the luxury of Potiphar's palace and goes on to be the best prisoner. Later, he goes on to be the best manager of the prisoners.... When he is released from prison, Joseph again decides to forget his past in prison and goes on to be the best in his new government position, a position which enables him to feed his father and brothers when they arrive from famine-struck Israel in search of food.

Although Joseph moved on from the past and forgave those he needed to forgive, he also remembered the past for its examples of God's goodness and redemption. Saying, "God has made me forget all my trouble and all my father's household" (Genesis 41:51), Joseph named his first son Manasseh, meaning "one who causes to forget." Later, saying, "God has made me fruitful in the land of my affliction" (verse 52), Joseph named his second son Ephraim, meaning "fruitful." Joseph moved on from the past and so was able to bear fruit in the present. He bloomed where he was planted, and God blessed him greatly.

Perhaps you—like Joseph at one time and like me the year we lived in nine different places—find yourself living where you don't want to be. Many times, like Joseph, we are not where we used to be and not where we want to be. And many times, like Joseph, we find ourselves holding positions or having responsibilities we did not choose for ourselves. In times like these, we can follow Joseph's example and forget the past, forgive those who have caused us pain, and focus on the present place and time, expecting our gracious God to work goodness and redemption in the circumstances. By determining to be the best we can be wherever we are, each one of us can bloom where we are planted.

So where has God placed you? Are you a missionary in Africa living in a mud hut or a widow living in a palatial but empty home? Are you in a rural community of 39 people or a metropolis of millions? Wherever He puts us, God has a purpose. Whatever the situation, it is an opportunity to bear fruit for His kingdom. However difficult the circumstances, He enables us to accomplish something for Him as long as we are looking to Him and making ourselves available to be used by Him.

While difficult and painful circumstances may make it difficult for us to pursue excellence as we serve God, circumstances which are too comfortable can have the same effect. We can become women who merely exist rather than women who serve God. Content with where we are, we don't press forward toward Christlike maturity.

My husband told me last week about one such woman who lives on a lake in middle America and thoroughly enjoys the quiet setting and leisurely pace. Her husband has a career opportunity that would bring him to Los Angeles, but she has no desire to relocate, especially to Los Angeles. I wonder if she mistakenly thinks "the prize" is to reside on waterfront property instead of the spiritual maturity that comes with forgetting the past, reaching forward, and pressing ahead toward "the upward call of God in Christ Jesus" (Philippians 3:14). Leaving her lake would mean taking a risk, making a move, and growing her faith through those changes. In this woman's case, her comfort seems to be causing her faith to stop growing.

Again, Paul warns us against resting on past achievements or present comfort. He urges us to purposefully look ahead and reach forward, to continue in the race and discover a deeper faith in God. For growth to occur, there must be tension in our life. That healthy, productive tension comes from goals we set with God's guidance and from our decision to be the best we can be for Him wherever we are. That healthy tension, which means for us a growing faith, does not come when we are too comfortable. Too much comfort invites us to watch the race rather than to energetically participate in it.

Whether we, like Joseph, find ourselves in a difficult situation or, like the woman living by the lake, are enjoying a life of comfort utterly void of challenge, we must resolve to focus on God's purpose for us. We must choose to pursue His will for us and, strengthened by Him, participate in the race He calls us to run. Again, whether we are experiencing pain or pleasure right now, we need Paul's mindset—"One thing I do: forgetting what lies behind and reaching forward to what lies ahead, I press on toward the goal for the prize of the upward call of God in Christ Jesus" (Philippians 3:13-14).

A Heart and a Mind for God

When we choose to forget the past (as we've defined "forget"), seek God's purpose in our life, and decide to be the best we can be for Him wherever we find ourselves, we will be very focused people. And focus is essential to running the race. If a runner fails to focus, that runner fails. But focus—in an Olympic race or our Christian walk—does not always come easily. Every time I sit down to read the Bible, I suddenly think of all the things I need to do—not only today but for the rest of my life! I fight the urge to jump up and move the clothes from the washer to the dryer, or I think of a person I need to call and instinctively reach for the phone. It is a battle to focus my mind and my heart on reading the Bible and praying. So I go to war.

The conversation I have with myself goes something like this: "No, I'll write that down and do it later. I'm going to read my Bible. . . . No, I'll call her later. I'm going to read my Bible. . . . I'll let my answering machine take that call. That's why I have it. I'm going to read my Bible. . . . I'm not going to put the clothes in the dryer right now because I'll need to be there when they finish drying. I don't want that kind of pressure right now. I'm going to read my Bible. . . . I'll write that letter later. I'll load the dishwasher later. I'll make the bed later. I'll call the repairman later. *I'm going to read my Bible!*"

It can feel like a real battle, but it's not a battle I fight alone. After all, my heavenly Father, who desires this time of fellowship with me, is also the Victor over Satan who would distract me from these moments of sweet communion with Him. While it helps me to imagine myself wearing mental blinders that make it impossible to see all the options available to me, even more compelling is God's gracious love for me. So I ask God to help me focus on Him. I lift before Him my struggle and the concerns and duties that crowd in. I ask His gracious presence to be with me as I seek to fix my heart and mind on Him and Him alone. When I ask God to clear my mind of all that is interfering with our time together, He grants me peace. He enables me to be with Him so that I can receive His love and then go through the day loving Him with all my heart, soul, and mind. True to the promise of Isaiah 26:3—"The steadfast of mind Thou wilt keep in perfect peace"—God does indeed help us fix our heart and mind on Him.

A Vigilant, Steady Focus

Throughout our busy days, whatever situations come our way, God will help us keep our eyes on Him. I remember one morning when I received a telephone call from a woman who was upset with me—"You said this . . . and then you did that . . . and I don't think you should have. . . ." I hear critical comments about a lot of things, but this time the attack was personal.

As I was listening to this woman, I also heard the front door open and a familiar "Yahoo!" My daughter Courtney stuck her smiling face around the corner of my office door and waved. She had stopped by to pick up a few papers from her files. Because Courtney lives on The Master's College campus, every moment with her is a blessing.

I explained (I hope graciously) to the caller that my daughter had just stopped by and arranged to finish our talk later. As I hung up the phone, I noticed my increased heart rate and my churning stomach. I was feeling bewildered, confused, hurt, and angry. I wanted to process all that had been said and deal with the situation, but here was my lovely daughter, chattering away as I fixed us a snack. Courtney was here, Courtney was now, and Courtney was real. The phone call was already thirty seconds in the past.

Was I going to let a negative phone call—that was over and done with—ruin my time with my daughter? She was my next assignment from God. Realizing that being with Courtney was God's will for me now, I decided to turn my focus forward. I decided to be the best mother I could be at that moment. That meant "forgetting" the call and going on by focusing on my daughter. So I riveted my eyes on her and listened intently. I chose to savor the present, precious moments with my daughter.

My focus changed from the phone call to my daughter, and such changes in focus are part of the rhythm of life. Although our primary focus on God and His presence with us remains the same, our focus on the details of life changes as we go about the events of our day. That ultimate focus, however, enables us to put aside any unpleasantness or pain to deal with later so that we can experience and enjoy whatever is happening in the present. After all, the demands of the present—the tasks to perform, the duties to fulfill, the responsibilities to handle, the people to meet—comprise the course on which we run the race toward Christlikeness.

And, as we run that race, many voices call us to abandon the effort. The world woos us away from following Christ and offers tempting rewards for choosing its way to what it deems success. We feel pressure to be like people in the neighborhood or at the office, and we aren't always affirmed in our efforts toward excellence. The past would hold us prisoner, chained and bound to darker days and deeds, and the flesh calls us to have some fun, take it easy, don't worry, and take care of it tomorrow. The world doesn't understand the Christian's race and the prize that awaits. The world doesn't acknowledge the cause of Christ or value the commitment His cause requires.

Despite the din of these various voices, the runner who is looking ahead and reaching forward has ears for only one voice. The runner clearly hears God's strong voice over the weaker but persistent voices of the world that call us to lesser pursuits and duller prizes. Through the pages of Scripture, God's strong voice urges us to go on and offers us the encouragement we need as we serve Him. God's Word calls us to look ahead, to determine our God-given purpose, to set our sights on the goals He gives us, to be the best we can be for Him, to daily fix both heart and mind on God Himself, and to direct our focus forward every minute. God's Word tells us to go on—and God's Word reassures us that He is with us as we run the race, offering guidance and strength each step of the way.

Discouraging voices will be loud and persuasive, as Christopher Columbus experienced on his journey across the Atlantic. Day after day he sailed without seeing land, and again and again his sailors threatened mutiny. They tried to persuade him to turn back, but Columbus refused to listen. Each day he entered in the ship's log the two words, "Sailed on." Those are the two words we need to enter into the log of our journey. We need to sail on as we look ahead and reach forward toward spiritual maturity and the goal of loving God with all our mind. As we focus on God, He will guide our steps, empower our service to Him, and work in us the characteristics of Christ as He enables us to both meet the demands of the present and, as the next chapter explains, press on toward the the prize.

7

Keeping On
Keeping On

———— ❧ ————

I press on toward the goal for the prize
of the upward call of God in Christ Jesus.
Philippians 3:14

———— ❧ ————

When my husband was employed by a pharmaceutical company, his district manager was known among his sales force for a certain saying. No matter what happened, his words were always the same: "Keep on keeping on." If Jim did well or won the district sales contest, he was told, "Keep on keeping on." If Jim's sales fell or he lost an important account, he was again told, "Keep on keeping on." Whether Jim excelled or failed, neither was to slow his progress. He was to keep on keeping on. Paul advocates this same attitude in Philippians 3:14 when he writes, "I press on toward the goal for the prize of the upward call of God in Christ Jesus."

First, having forgotten the past—having learned from our experiences and remembering God's faithfulness but holding loosely the good and the bad which would keep us from growing on our walk of faith—we then turned our face toward Jesus and focused on Him. In our race toward becoming like Christ and loving God with all our mind, we began reaching for that goal by focusing on the present. As one commentator observed, "We must look forward, not backward. Some men stand with their faces to the west, regretting the lost radiance of the setting sun. Others turn their gaze on the east, eager to catch the first streak of dawn. Surely the latter are the wiser. Our faces look forwards that we may see the path we are about to tread."[1] As we experience God's love more fully, we look to the dawning of fresh opportunities to learn from Him and to show our love for Him by serving Him. We also choose to invest our energy on progress rather than on the faded events of the past.

Having assumed this runner's posture ("reaching forward" in the present), we now begin the pursuit by "[pressing] on toward the goal for the prize of the upward call of God in Christ Jesus" (Philippians 3:14). Just as a marathon runner presses on to finish the race, so you and I must settle for nothing less than living every day of our life for Jesus. To quote the title of Oswald Chambers' well-known devotional, doing so means giving "my utmost for His Highest."[2] "Pressing on" means running "with utmost effort"[3] and suggests "active and earnest endeavor."[4] We are to "strain every nerve to pursue the ideal,"[5] but, as we noted earlier, we are to draw on God's grace and strength each step of the way.

This pursuit of the ideal, this pressing on toward the goal, is a race we will run for the rest of our life. Such effort can only be extended to something significant, and the motivation and perseverance needed will come only if the purpose is grand enough. That "something significant" is the Savior who died for us, and focusing on Jesus will enable us to give our wholehearted effort to the race of life. We can only keep on keeping on when we have our eyes on Him, our crucified and risen Lord.

A Grand Purpose

As we talked about in the previous chapter, purpose is paramount. I know I can't do anything, including get out of bed on time, without having a sense of God's purpose for my life. Knowing my purpose—knowing that I am here to give my life in service to God and His people—is a driving motivator in this race toward Christ-likeness called life, and this supreme purpose keeps me keeping on.

It is important, however, to develop specific goals for yourself under this broad aim of serving God with your life. When my husband conducts goal-setting seminars for men, he asks the men to write at the top of a sheet of paper, "What are your lifetime goals?" They are then to answer that question by writing without stopping until Jim's timer rings. Once they stop writing, they spend a few more minutes fine-tuning their answers. Then Jim has the participants choose the three goals which are most important and rank them in order from most important to least important. This exercise enables each person to articulate what he wants to do with his life.

I remember well the first goal-setting seminar Jim led. It was for the two of us one Sunday afternoon. We had spent a glorious and uplifting morning at church being taught, stretched, and challenged. Inspired by the worship and full of wishes and dreams, we knew we wanted to love Christ better and serve Him in some greater way. He had saved our souls, blessed our marriage and family, and given our lives purpose. Now what could we do for Him?

This conference-for-two was held in our home. As Jim and I sat facing each other at the dining table, we worked through these few simple exercises that would change us forever. The desires of our full hearts spilled out on paper as we penned our responses. Little did we know that something as simple as the question "What are my lifetime goals?" could be the catalyst for grand goals that would energize us for the rest of our lives. We were—and still are—willing and enthusiastic about pressing toward those goals which are enabling us to fulfill the purpose of our life: serving Jesus Christ.

What three goals did I define for myself that day? First, to be a supportive and encouraging wife and mother; second, to be a woman of God growing in my knowledge of and love for Him and enabling others to do so; and, third, to teach the Bible so that women's lives are changed. Since setting those lifetime goals almost 20 years ago, I have known not only the purpose of my life, but the purpose for each day. Although I will never completely reach these goals, they challenge me daily to be the best I can be for God. These goals have kept me on track through the years and encouraged me to keep on keeping on.

Are you focused on a specific yet grand purpose for your life? Can you, like Paul, talk about the "one thing" you do (Philippians 3:13)? While it's good to think and dream about what you want to do for Christ, it's essential to articulate specific lifetime goals that, as you work toward them, will enable you to fulfill your purpose of serving God. Seeing your goals written out on paper will be sobering as you consider the privilege of working for God's kingdom and that high calling of your daily life. Those goals will also be very motivating as they remind you that you can, by the grace of God, do something eternally significant with your days on this earth.

If you haven't yet made personal your God-given purpose of serving Him by establishing specific goals for your life, I encourage you to take the next hour to do so. Close the bedroom door, go to a coffee shop on your lunch hour, or clear the breakfast dishes off the kitchen table after everyone leaves and spend sixty minutes with God thinking and praying about His goals for your life. Answer the question, "What are your lifetime goals?" Then select from your list the three goals that are most significant to you and rank them in order of importance. You won't be the same after this hour with your Lord, pondering His purposes for you. I guarantee that you will discover new dimensions to your life and new energy for God's calling as you glimpse all that you can be and do for Christ and in Him.

A Concerted Effort

Once you have set your goals for your lifelong pursuit of serving God, you will undoubtedly want to do your best and give your all to achieve those goals. Like Paul, you will want to press on and hold nothing back. Such pressing on, however, is "untiring activity"[6] which requires perseverance, and that perseverance is a gift of God's grace available to us all. And it is God's grace that keeps the kind of woman I'm describing from being a breathless, harried, frazzled female. Instead, as one of God's servants, she depends on His guidance and His strength as she presses on. She walks through her days sensitized to His presence and trusting in His perfect timing. She keeps moving, keeps serving, keeps functioning, keeps growing, keeps giving, and keeps pressing on toward her goals of serving God—but her movement is not frenzied or compulsive. Willing to work hard and persevere for her Lord, she draws strength from Him and focuses her energy and efforts on her goals, balancing her efforts with the knowledge that God is God and that He is ultimately in control.

"Wings As Eagles"

As we face forward and press on, we are to remember that we do not need to rely solely on our own efforts in the race. Hear the promise of Isaiah 40:31—"Those who wait for the LORD will gain new strength; they will mount up with wings like eagles, they will run and not get tired, they will walk and not become weary." God is there to enable us to serve Him wherever He has called us to do so.

I hope you have experienced days when mounting up with wings like an eagle and pressing on seem effortless and enjoyable as you soar with God. But perhaps you have also experienced the kind of day that prompted Amy Carmichael, pioneer missionary to India, to pray, "Father, I'm not soaring today. Help me." Our heavenly Father responded, "Daughter, soaring is not always flying high above the world. Sometimes one is soaring only two feet above the ground, just enough to keep you from getting tangled in the thorns and crashing against the rocks."[7]

Some days we may feel that we are soaring awfully close to the rocks. We may feel too tired to run, and our walk may not be much more than a limp or a stagger. Again, we keep facing forward. (As the chief research scientist of General Motors noted, "The enthusiast fails forward"!)[8] When you and I weaken and even "fail forward," we are to remember that God is ultimately in control to use us for His end in His time and in His way. Resting in Him and relying on Him, we can keep on keeping on whatever obstacles and distractions arise. Pressing on is our duty and, as one commentator wisely points out, "We are not blamed if we have not yet reached that crown of goodness. But we are blamed if we are not pressing on to it and rest contented with anything short of it."[9]

Focusing on the Goal

Paul kept pressing on, and one reason he was able to do so was his focus on the goal: The primary aim of his life was to finish the race. Have you made the decision to press forward for Christ until the end of your life? I have to admit that, when I first became a Christian, I had not made that decision. I daydreamed instead of the world's ideal goal for my life—retirement. I looked forward to living at the beach and enjoying travel, cruises, walking, reading, and dabbling in various hobbies. At a certain time, I thought, Jim and I would quit working and together live out the fantasies pictured on the brochures and maps I had collected.

My husband, however, had very different ideas! Jim firmly told me, "I'm never going to retire." With that statement, my daydreams vaporized and I recognized God's plan for His people. I realized that living for Christ means living for Him all the way to the end. We are called to live for Christ every day of our life, not until some magical, arbitrary age when we stop serving others and serve only ourselves. We are called to finish the race.

And finishing the race isn't always easy. Sometimes along the way we may have to follow the example of the ice skaters my family and I watched during the 1992 winter Olympics. We watched the competition—but we certainly didn't relax and enjoy the skating. Instead, holding our breaths and biting our nails, we endured the skating. During both the women's and men's events, I kept thinking, "If anyone just stays standing, they're going to win the gold medal!" Every single skater fell, and what happened after each fall was, for me, more spectacular than the skating feats. Each skater got up and went on. One skater even fell three times, got up three times, and went on to finish.

The best ice skaters in the world were falling. Every one of them fell—and every one of them got up and finished. During their long years of training, they had learned to always get up and finish the competition. They had learned, among other things, to keep on keeping on. Because they did so, they were indeed winners.

In fact, when the medals were presented at the Olympics, each one was awarded to a skater who had fallen, gotten up, and finished. We are to do the same.

People of the Bible Who Focused to the End

Retirement from the Christian life is not in God's plan. As you turn through the pages of Scripture, you can't find one saint who quit. Although many wanted to (remember Elijah, Jonah, and David?), not one did. Consider the following roll call of saints.

- Throughout his life, Abraham responded to God's commands to move. He lived in tents, his nomad's life representing his search for "the city . . . whose architect and builder is God" (Hebrews 11:10). Abraham died without receiving the fulfillment of God's promises of land, a vast number of descendants, and great blessing (see Genesis 12:1-3 and Hebrews 11:39). Abraham could have quit, but he desired "a better country, that is a heavenly one" (Hebrews 11:16). So, until he died, Abraham pressed on.

- Aged and weary, Moses kept serving the Lord. At one point, he even needed the help of Aaron and Hur to hold his hands up so that God would continue to bless the Israelites' efforts in battle (Exodus 17:8-13). He could have quit, but he didn't. Instead, he got the help he needed to raise his hands heavenward. Later, because Moses hadn't obeyed and trusted God for water at Meribah (see Numbers 20:9-13), God forbade him to cross into the Promised Land he had waited 40 years to enter. Again, Moses could have quit serving God, but he didn't. Instead, he spent the rest of his days teaching the law, preparing the priests, and encouraging Joshua to lead God's people into the land his feet would never touch.

• Samuel was called by God to be His prophet, but later the people of Israel rejected his leadership and asked him to appoint a king over them so that they would be like their neighboring nations (1 Samuel 8:1-5). Most people quit after being rejected, but Samuel didn't. Instead, he kept praying and preaching (12:23), and he spent the rest of his life helping Saul, the man who took his place as the leader of the nation.

• King David greatly desired to build a temple to God, but the Lord Almighty said to David, "You have shed much blood, and have waged great wars; you shall not build a house to My name, because you have shed so much blood on the earth before Me" (1 Chronicles 22:8). But instead of quitting, David kept pressing on for the Lord. He spent his last days making plans and gathering materials so that his son Solomon could build the temple (1 Chronicles 22:5-19).

• Paul spent his final days writing letters from prison which would guide the church of Jesus Christ in the future. His impending death didn't shift his sharp focus on Jesus Christ and His people. He kept pressing on to the end of his life by offering encouragement, exhortation, and comfort through his pen.

• Exiled to the island of Patmos in his old age, the apostle John could have quit. After all, his service for Christ had seemingly earned him only disgrace and dishonor. But John kept pressing on. In his nineties, he was blessed with "the Revelation of

Jesus Christ" (Revelation 1:1). The twenty-two chapters of the Book of Revelation tell what will take place before and when the Lord returns. The apostle served as prophet with words that still speak to us today.

• Jesus Christ knew about the cross, but He pressed on toward it and, when it was time, He endured it to the end (Hebrews 12:2). As He hung dying on that cruel instrument of torture to save you and me from our sins, He uttered the three simple words, "It is finished" (John 19:30). Jesus, our Savior and our Lord, pressed on to the end.

The list of God's people who pressed on and served the Lord until the end of their life goes on and on. At one time or another as they ran the race, each of the men of faith mentioned above had a valid reason to quit. People told them, "No!" God told them, "No!" Circumstances seemed to scream, "No!" Yet not one of them quit, resigned, or retired. They knew they hadn't finished the race, that there was more work to be done, and that God could still use them. They knew that, by God's grace, they could make a difference for His kingdom right up until the day they left this earth and went to be with Him. They kept on keeping on.

While God may not have called you and me to achieve anything near the magnitude of these men's accomplishments, He does view our sphere of service and responsibility as equally important. God, for instance, has called me to press on in my service as a wife, a mother, and a teacher at church, and the examples of David, Paul, and the others encourage me to reach forward daily and to press on to the end. These saints had a clear vision of God which inspired them in their calling—and now inspires me in mine—to press on toward the end in service of the Almighty.

People in Our Time Who Focused to the End

Examples that instruct us and inspire us to keep on keeping on are available in our time as well as in the Bible. Two women have especially modeled for me the kind of faith and love for God that keeps us pressing on "toward the goal for the prize of the upward call of God in Christ Jesus." First is Corrie Ten Boom.

In *The Five Silent Years of Corrie Ten Boom*, her assistant and companion Pamela Rosewell writes about Corrie's ministry during the last five years of her life. When she was 86, Corrie suffered two debilitating strokes that left her unable to speak and barely able to move. Nevertheless, until her death at age 91, she received visitors, interceded in prayer for others, and, by doing so, modeled to everyone in her presence, her trust in and love for God. Although her ministry moved from public to private, from platform to pallet, from preaching to praying, Corrie Ten Boom pressed on to the end.[10]

The other woman whose example has greatly encouraged me is Shirley Price, teacher and creator of the curriculum piece entitled *God's Plan for the Wife and Mother*.[11] She delivered her final messages on Wednesday mornings in late 1974 at First Baptist Church of Van Nuys, California. Although undergoing radiation and chemotherapy for the cancer that would take her life on January 29, 1975, Shirley pressed on and finished those eight sessions which would help countless Christian wives and mothers. I was one of those recipients who later benefited from her tapes and materials. Focused on her goal of serving Jesus and His people, Shirley pressed on.

Women who are focused on "the prize of the upward call of God in Christ Jesus" know that it awaits them at the end of the race. Although minor rewards may come along the way, the highest honor doesn't come until we've run the entire race. So, acting on our love for Him, we are to press on and serve God every day of our life. Then we will receive that prize as we see face-to-face the Lord who Himself endured to the end.

Running Unencumbered

The writer to the Hebrews knows what Paul knows—and what you have probably realized—about running the race. Hear his exhortation: "Let us also lay aside every encumbrance, and the sin which so easily entangles us, and let us run with endurance the race that is set before us" (Hebrews 12:1). Running the race is easier when we aren't weighted down by sin.

Consider for a moment how you're doing in this leg of the race. I regularly use the following questions to evaluate my race: What habits, thought patterns, or activities are holding you back or slowing you down? What goals are keeping your pursuit of God from being the most important activity in your life? What messages from the world seem to be drowning out God's call to you? What do you need to lay aside so that you can better serve God?

I asked my husband what, through the years, he has had to lay aside in order to run the race and serve the Lord. Jim laughed and said, "Always television and food!" He knows that excess in these two areas is an encumbrance for him and looks to God to help him be discerning and moderate about both.

Take your own inventory of things that keep you from giving your whole heart to the race God has called you to run. By laying aside the useless, the wasteful, the meaningless, and the unimportant that can clutter our lives, we will be freer to serve God with all our being.

A Look in the Mirror

Read again Paul's words in Philippians 3:13-14— "Forgetting what lies behind and reaching forward to what lies ahead, I press on toward the goal for the prize of the upward call of God in Christ Jesus." These are the words of a man who knows the purpose of his life and who is focused on that goal. Have you, like Paul, determined your purpose in Christ? If so, are you doing your best to serve God and experiencing His grace as you try? Are you keeping your eyes on Jesus and letting your vision of Him inspire you along the way? Are you committed to keep on keeping on to the end of your life? And are you unencumbered as you "press on toward the goal for the prize of the upward call of God in Christ Jesus"?

We who name Christ "Lord" and "Savior" are called to love Him with all our heart, soul, and mind. This command gives our life purpose, richness, and a significance which commentator William Barclay describes like this: "To know Christ means that we share the way He walked; we share the Cross He bore; we share the death He died; and finally we share the life He lives for evermore."[12]

The Halfway Point

Having read this chapter, you are now more than halfway through this discussion of loving God with all your mind. So far, the book has emphasized the practical and the day-to-day. After all, life is lived one day at a time. We run the race for God and serve Him and His people wherever He has called us to be. For that reason, what we do in our daily routine truly has eternal significance. And this daily routine is the arena where we experience God's love and learn to love Him with all our mind.

So, at this halfway point, consider how God has been at work in your life to change the way you think. Is He, for instance, clearing your mind of some of the things which once interfered with your loving Him? More specifically, is He helping you think on what is true and real—His love, His provision, His ways, and His timing in your life—rather than on "if onlys" and "what ifs" (chapters 1 and 2)? With His help, are you addressing the concerns of today, knowing that today is all you can do anything about and therefore finding yourself less anxious (chapters 3 and 4)? Trusting in God and leaving your past in His hands, are you forgetting the good as well as the bad which would keep you from serving Him wholeheartedly today? Finally, are you looking ahead, reaching forward, and pressing on toward Christ by serving Him wherever He has placed you?

If you can answer yes to one or more of these questions, be encouraged by how God is transforming you into the image of His Son. As you continue to experience God's transforming love and find yourself loving Him more in return, you will experience a deeper, richer relationship with your Lord. And that relationship is key to a fulfilling life. After all, it is God's love that keeps us focused on the eternal and spiritual aspect of all that we do.

In fact, in one of my favorite "Cathy" cartoons, Cathy's mother offers her daughter some advice about focus. As Cathy and her mother shop in the mall, Cathy laments, "Behind me all I see is a trail of relationship blunders." Mother sagely replies, "Don't look back, Cathy."

Next Cathy complains, "Above me all I see are balloons, and when I look down I see that they are attached to strollers full of babies that aren't mine." Again Mother advises, "Don't look up. Don't look down."

Cathy then cries, "Ahead of me all I see is the most romantic day of the year—Valentine's Day—and no man." Mother summarizes, "Don't look back, up, down or ahead."

With her eyes covered, Cathy says, "Now I can't see anything at all." Mother comes through again, "Trust me, life is less confusing this way."[13]

Like Cathy, we can't follow her mother's advice. We are not to go through life with blinders on. We are to have our eyes open and focused on Christ. If we aren't focused on Him, life will indeed be confusing. Our focus on Jesus, our relationship with Him, and our commitment to serving Him as best we can as long as we live give significance and purpose to our life.

But, as I've mentioned again and again in these first seven chapters, our efforts to serve God and to think on what is real, live for today, forget the past, and focus fully on the present are not things we are supposed to be able to do on our own. This call to love God with all your mind is a call to experience God's grace—to receive from Him a new sensitivity to His presence in your life, strength for what He has called you to do, and joy in getting to know Him better as you walk with Him every minute of every day. After all, how could you help but love the One who gives your life purpose, who enables you to fulfill that purpose, and who promises the reward of life eternal with Him when you finish running the race?

8

Trusting the Lord

---

*We know that God causes all things
to work together for good . . .*
Romans 8:28

It was the day of our monthly committee meeting. Eager to plan future events for the women of the church, our leadership group had gathered in the Fireside Room, but something was wrong. Our chairman, who had reminded each of us about the meeting, wasn't there. After waiting for several minutes, we started the meeting without her. Later, as we neared our dismissal time, Bonnie calmly arrived, smiling broadly and announcing that she had experienced "another opportunity to trust the Lord."

Earlier that day, at the public park, one of her four children had disappeared. Bonnie told us of her initial panic and near-crippling emotions. In order to think clearly enough to deal with the situation, she had focused on God instead of listening to her raging emotions. Her conversation with herself went like this: "Was God in control? Yes. Did God know where her son was? Of course. Was God able to take care of him? Definitely. Could God help her? Certainly."

As Bonnie turned her turbulent thoughts to God and considered His presence, His power, His knowledge, and His involvement in her life, she was able to logically and systematically develop a plan of action for finding her son. She also followed the lessons taught in the first three Scripture passages we've looked at. Bonnie thought on what was real, not any what ifs or if onlys (Philippians 4:8). She dealt with this assignment from God as it arrived and relied on Him to meet the challenge (Matthew 6:34). And, leaning on God, she focused on the present until the emergency was over (Philippians 3:13,14).

"Another opportunity to trust the Lord" seems to arise almost daily for many of us. The three passages we've already looked at can help us when such an opportunity presents itself, and so can Romans 8:28, the verse we'll look at in this chapter and the next.

Knowing God

When Bonnie told the leadership committee about her experience, I saw that she was able to face the frightening situation because she knew God and His great love for her and her son. Bonnie knew God well enough to be able to trust Him. Her knowledge of God gave her hope, and that kind of knowing God determines our view of life and how we approach the challenges of each day.

So, as we begin the second half of this book, you'll notice a shift from the practicalities of daily life to an emphasis on God. If we are to live in close relationship with God as He desires and serve Him and His people as He has called us to, we must, as one pastor observed, "see God as the God of the Bible—supreme, sovereign, and sensitive. . . . The Christian life is kept fine-tuned by biblical theology. We should always interpret experience by truth—we should always filter every pain through the lens of deity. When God is in sharp focus, then life is also undistorted."[1]

When God is in sharp focus for us, we are a step closer to loving Him with all our mind. God also uses these biblically sound thoughts to help us respond to the events in our life calmly, rationally, and with hope because we know Him. In fact, when we acknowledge God's supreme role in our life and set our mind on Him, He enables us to be women of hope.

Knowing God the Father

Have you ever met a woman with bright eyes and a ready smile whose positive outlook on life gives her contagious energy? Her secret may be knowing that God's great love for her means that everything that happens to her—in the present as well as the past and the future—will be for the good in the hands of her heavenly Father. This kind of woman is confident that God watches over every aspect of her life, and she greets every event with this knowledge. Her enthusiasm for life is rooted in her knowledge of the God who gives us the promise of Romans 8:28.

In the Book of Romans, the apostle Paul thoroughly and powerfully presents the doctrine of justification by faith. In chapter 8, Paul affirms the blessed position of those of us who name Jesus as Lord and Savior and, by virtue of His death for our sins, are accepted by God as His children. Paul then offers believers hope and comfort in present trials as he explains that the very trials which threaten us are actually "overruled" by God.[2] As Paul himself writes, "God causes all things to work together for good to those who love God." This truth of Romans 8:28, a verse much loved by many Christians, gives us knowledge of God which bears the fruit of hope in our life.

Knowing God Is at Work

I met with a woman to talk about some problems in her life that were not going away. As she spoke, her tale turned to her childhood and the extreme poverty and backwardness of her early home. It didn't take me long to see, however, that she was allowing these past circumstances, as difficult as they were, to affect her present situation—and was blaming God for both.

Whenever tough times come our way, we may find ourselves falling into that same trap of thinking that God made a mistake or that He wasn't there when we needed Him, thoughts which can rob us of our hope. The Bible, however, describes a God who is perfect in His wisdom, His ways, and His timing, a God who is with us always, and a God who loves us. During our tough times, God comforts us with His presence and through the biblical truths that He was and is with us always, that He doesn't make mistakes, and that He is always in control. He reminds us that He, the Divine Designer, knows what He is doing and that our history, whatever our experience, is not an error, but a part of His plan. Reminded that God is in control and, rather than trying to reconcile some of the harsher aspects of reality (incest, cancer, airplane crashes, victims of drunk drivers, etc.) with that truth, acknowledging that His ways aren't our ways, we can face life with hope in Him.

So what could the woman I was counseling with do—and what can you and I do—to be more sensitive to God's presence in our lives? The following three steps have helped me.

Step #1: List the negatives in your life. Your list may include your background, your parents (or lack of them), your siblings, your appearance, your abilities, your personality, your marital status, your children (or lack of them), your finances, and whatever challenges you may currently face.

Step #2: Acknowledge God in the negatives. God knew, God allowed, God planned, and God permitted. As Romans 8:28 states, "God causes all things [including the things you don't like about your life] to work together for [*your*] good."

Step #3: Thank God for each negative. More specifically, thank Him for being able to work for your good and for your spiritual growth in everything in your life you don't like. Remember that God has designed your life (Psalm 139:13-16), that He has a plan for your life (2 Timothy 1:9), and that He is actively working out His will through the people, events, and circumstances of your life—past, present, and future. There has never been a mistake and there never has been or ever will be a second where God is not present with you, superintending and being actively involved in your life. Acknowledging that God has planned your life can help free you from bitterness and resentment toward people, events, and circumstances and give you hope. A woman of hope is a woman who knows that God is the Author of every moment of her life.

Knowing God Works All Things Together

A woman of hope also knows that God "works together" all things—the bad, the good, the unexpected, the seemingly coincidental, the moments we are an innocent victim, and the times we are guilty of sin. Because He is God, He is able to weave together every single aspect and event in your life and produce something good. Because He is God, He causes everything in your life "to cooperate to the furtherance and final completion of His high design."[3] Because He is God, He is able to overrule all of the evil in your life and cause it to work together for good.[4]

I thought about this marvelous promise one day while I was in the kitchen. At the risk of trivializing the hope of Romans 8:28, I want you to think about making a chocolate cake. You begin with bitter chocolate. Then you stir in some dry, tasteless flour. Next come raw eggs and some sour milk. When you thoroughly mix these and several more ingredients and bake the batter in a hot oven, the end result is a lovely chocolate cake.

Now think about your life—the bitter, the dry, the raw, the sour, the heat. In God's hands, these things will result in something good. The hope of Romans 8:28 is that, in God's hands, the ingredients of our lives will always work out for our good and His eternal purposes. Let this promise encourage you the next time you are facing the bitterness, the sourness, or the heat of life. Know that God is in control.

Knowing God Uses All Things

God is in control of all things. There is no fine print to that promise. There are no disclaimers. Everything—every event, every person, all of the past, all of the present, all of the future—falls under God's jurisdiction.

All things includes the most pressing problem you currently face. Fill in the blank: "My number-one problem is _____." Each day I identify the greatest challenge I face and then acknowledge that God has promised to work that very thing for good in my life. My outlook on that problem changes when I remind myself of God's promise to turn something very bad—the worst thing in my life—into something good. Romans 8:28 points me to God and gives me hope for the day ahead.

All things includes good things. Ministry opportunities, a promotion at work, a move to a different city, graduation from college, and a new job are some good things which God can use to spark new growth in us. Each of these good things—and others you would add to the list—carries with it a degree of challenge as you do something you have never done before. When you are tempted to feel flustered or frustrated by new and challenging circumstances, remember your powerful, good God and His promise to you. He causes the good things in your life to work together for good as you learn new skills and grow to greater levels of faithfulness, wisdom, and trust.

One good thing which God uses in the lives of many women to cause us to grow is a baby, a fact I recalled as I was making phone calls to invite our staff wives to a spring luncheon. One of our women had brought her first baby home from the hospital two days earlier. As I was dialing Dina's number, I thought back to my own first days of motherhood—and put the phone down. I decided to call her a few days later after she'd had a little more time to adjust. A baby is indeed a miracle, a precious gift from God, and a very good thing in our life, but any mother you talk to will tell you that a baby causes a woman to stretch and grow like nothing else in her life. Being a mother truly is an assignment from God which He uses, for instance, to make us more Christlike by giving us countless opportunities to die to our self. God does indeed use the good of a child for our good and for our growth in Him.

All things includes bad things. The world is full of tragedy, pain, evil, suffering, and heartache, but Romans 8:28 teaches us that God uses even these bad things for our good. And if God promises to cause such bad things to work together for our good, then there can be no completely bad things. This truth can be a source of comfort and hope in the face of the inexplicable occurrences and tragedies of life.

And inexplicable occurrences and tragedies happen. Women have come to me burdened by the death of a child, a difficult pregnancy, unemployment, rape, estranged family members, divorce, infertility, and cancer. We can also be disturbed by an angry phone caller, a friend's snub, a misunderstanding, or a canceled vacation. My pastor, John MacArthur, shared his insight on these bad things in his commentary: "Paul is not saying that God prevents His children from experiencing things that can harm them. He is rather attesting that the Lord takes all that He allows to happen to His beloved children, even the worst things, and turns those things ultimately into blessings."[5] What a wonderful God we have!

All things includes large things. It was Wednesday night, and the weekly college Bible study was meeting in our family room. All week long, my husband had been helping Bryant, who was to teach that night on Romans 8:28. We saw the others stifle yawns of boredom as he read the familiar text. Quickly, however, all of us were drawn into Paul's message anew as this young man told about the large and bad thing that had happened to him.

Bryant described in graphic detail the car accident he had been in, his stay in the hospital, the amputation of his leg immediately below the hip, his recovery, his physical therapy, and the eventual finding and fitting of an artificial leg. He shared openly his feelings as he had struggled emotionally, physically, and practically to adjust to a new way of life. The path to an athletic scholarship was closed to him forever, and his plans for the future were undone by that tragic accident. As Bryant quietly explained how he had relied on Romans 8:28, with its powerful truth and its promise from God, that verse was brought to life for us.

How had God used the car accident and the loss of a leg for good in Bryant's life? First, Bryant explained, the hospital stay gave him time to take a spiritual inventory of his life and make a fresh commitment to God. During his stay in the hospital, he also took time to list the many reasons he still had for giving thanks to God. He reported that relationships with his family were strengthened as they gathered around him during the crisis. With the death of his athletic dreams, Bryant chose to concentrate on biblical theology. Because of the large, bad thing that happened to him, Bryant was now at a Christian college, a student body officer majoring in Bible, teaching a college Bible study, and aiming for seminary in preparation for a life of ministry to the God and Savior who saved not only his soul, but his life.

All things includes small things. While the bad in our life may not be on the scale of Bryant's experience, all of us have had experiences which we can only label "bad." These relatively small things can nevertheless cause the pearl of greater faith to take shape in our life as we see God act according to the promise of Romans 8:28. And, while I may be exceptionally sensitive, insults always have me turning to those words of hope.

One Sunday morning I was starting up the stairs at church. I had gotten up early to read my Bible, pray, and study the lesson I was going to teach the women's Sunday school class. I had just left the choir room after enjoying uplifting worship and an especially meaningful communion service. As I started up the stairs toward the classroom, a woman stopped to talk to me, and her words hurt me deeply.

Suddenly the benefits of my early-morning Bible study, prayer, and lesson preparation disappeared. Suddenly the joy of music, worship, and communion evaporated. Suddenly the newness and cleanness that had come with the confession of sins and the forgiveness we receive because of Christ's death was marred. I felt empty and hurt. How could I teach a lesson on God's grace and goodness right now?

I tried to do what I'd been learning about God and how to draw near to Him. First, I had to think about what was real. This woman really had said those hurtful words, but I chose not to go beyond her words in a quest for her motives or an incident when I might have offended her. I would deal only with her actual words.

But I would deal with them later. Right now I had to focus on the task at hand. Between the stairs and the classroom door—a distance I would cover in about forty-five seconds—I had to shift my sights to the lesson I was to teach. I asked the Lord to calm my thoughts and emotions, honor my earlier preparation, and use me to share a helpful message with the class.

I found hope when I turned to God in prayer during that forty-five-second walk. I prayed, "God, You knew from before the foundation of the world that on this morning at this time that woman would say those words to me. This incident is no surprise to You. In fact, You have sovereignly permitted it. Thank You for believing that I am able to handle this and thank You that You have promised to work this insult for good in my life." Through this prayer, God reminded me that He works insults as well as compliments for our good and our growth, and that truth gave me hope.

All things includes people. In the Old Testament, the story of Queen Esther offers an intriguing example of how God uses people in our life. Consider first the significant people in her life—her devoted uncle Mordecai, the helpful eunuch Hegai, her temperamental and distant husband, King Ahasuerus, and the evil villain Haman. An orphaned Jewish girl, Esther was raised by Mordecai. Later, when King Ahasuerus divorced his queen, this moody man chose Esther from among the women of his many provinces to become his queen. God used her position as queen to deliver His people from the plotting of their enemy Haman. Through the people He placed in Esther's life, God provided love, advice, and position to a girl without parents and, at the same time, accomplished His purposes in history.

Just as God used good as well as bad people for Esther's good and His purposes, He will do the same in your life. That truth offers great hope to the class I teach on Sunday mornings, a group of Christian women who are married to unbelieving husbands. In fact, I see the gentleness of these lovely, tempered, quiet, and accepting women as evidence that God is using their husbands to make them more Christlike. God is able to use the people who populate our life for our good. Whether the individual brings you joy or sorrow, pleasure or pain, comfort or conflict, he or she has come from the hand of God. He uses every single person in our life for our good and His purposes.

And a woman of hope can accept all people because she understands this truth. She can see her parents, her husband, her children, her supervisor, and even the angry stranger who yells at her from his car as part of all that God is using for good in her life. Furthermore, she refuses to treat any person differently than another because God made and loves all people. Finally, she acknowledges that good will come from every relationship, no matter how difficult or painful it is. Knowing that her loving Father is at work in her life frees her from resentment, bitterness, and blame.

As we have seen, *all things includes all things*. In his commentary on Romans, John F. MacArthur expands this thought: "No matter what our situation, our suffering, our persecution, our sinful failure, our pain, our lack of faith—in those things, as well as in *all* other *things*, our heavenly Father will work to produce our ultimate victory and blessing. The corollary of that truth is that nothing can ultimately work against us. Any temporary harm we suffer will be used by God for our benefit (see 2 Cor. 12:7-10). . . . *All things* includes circumstances and events that are good and beneficial in themselves as well as those that are in themselves evil and harmful."[6]

What all things in your life have in common—be they good or bad—is God's use of them for your good. This truth draws us nearer to God and sensitizes us to His presence in any and every situation. As nineteenth-century preacher and teacher D. L. Moody wrote in his personal Bible, "If our circumstances find us in God, we shall find God in all our circumstances."[7] When we look to the truth of Romans 8:28, we are "in God," and we find hope in Him.

And what honor we give to God when our thoughts about Him and His hand in our life are true! And what hope and encouragement the truth of Romans 8:28 brings to our aching soul! God has given us a promise, God controls all things, and God works all things for our good. We can therefore look at each one of the challenges and trials, the disappointments and tragedies of life as "another opportunity to trust the Lord." When our hope is in the Lord, we know that everything that happens to us—our most pressing problem, the good things, the bad things, the large things, the small things—will be used by God to bless us and make us more Christlike. With David, we can confidently proclaim, "Surely goodness . . . will follow me all the days of my life" (Psalm 23:6a).

Knowing God's Promise

Knowing God and trusting in His promise that He causes all things to work together for good makes us women of hope. This knowledge and this trust can also eliminate negative thoughts which would block our growth in the Lord and interfere with our daily duties.

Knowing the truth of Romans 8:28, for instance, reduces *doubt*. You may wonder why certain things happen and you may wonder why God seems so far away, but you need never wonder about His ability to make the events of your life work for your good and His purposes. As one translation of Romans 8:28 reads, "We know *with an absolute knowledge* that for those who are loving God, all things are working together resulting in good, for those who are called ones according to His purpose" (emphasis mine).[8]

Knowing Romans 8:28 also gives us truth to balance our *feelings*. A woman of hope rests in the promise that God will use everything which happens to her for good. She can therefore respond to good or bad situations with faith that her loving heavenly Father is already at work in the painful, the tragic, and the disappointing for His purposes and her good.

Knowing can prevent *bitterness*. Romans 8:28 gives us hope when we are hurt. A painful situation may feel and in fact be quite terrible, but God's promise is that good will come of it because He is at work in our life. This hope can keep the seeds of bitterness from taking root in our heart.

Knowing reduces such negative responses as *depression, discouragement, despair, defeat, anger, wrath, and frustration*. Some of those feelings may come, and it is not wise to deny and ignore them. But remembering Romans 8:28 and drawing close to God in faith, we can persevere, knowing that everything which happens is, in the hands of our loving God, ultimately good.

Knowing God and His promise in Romans 8:28 also eliminates the need for us to *manipulate* circumstances. Taking matters into our own hands when God is saying, "Wait," "Vengeance is mine," or "Not that way!" is evidence of our lack of trust in God. We can have something of a hands-off approach to life when we are trusting the truth of Romans 8:28, the promise that God causes all things to work together for good. After all, God is the Author of life. He knows what will happen beforehand, He enables us to cope and grow when hard times come, and He works good from bad. Therefore, leaving certain situations in God's hands is sometimes the best thing we can do and can indeed be a significant step of faith and hope.

The next time you experience the bad of life, remember the promise of Romans 8:28. Remind yourself that the God who loves you causes all things to work together for good, and He can use this truth to keep bitterness and negativism from taking root in your heart. So let that next trial be "another opportunity to trust the Lord." Then watch God keep His promise to you as He works in a situation for your good and His purposes.

As we've seen, in Romans 8:28, God makes us a promise, He reminds us that He is in control of all things, and He explains that He works all things for our good and His purposes. And, as we'll see in the next chapter, this powerful truth gives us three more reasons to hope.

9

Navigating the Maze of Life

———— ౭ล ————

We know that God causes all things
to work together for good
to those who love God,
to those who are called
according to His purpose.
Romans 8:28

———— ౭ล ————

The women from our church were crowded into a large conference room for our annual retreat. We were meeting at the headquarters of Campus Crusade for Christ in Arrowhead Springs, California, and our speaker was Ney Bailey from their staff. I still remember the story Ney told that first evening, a story which I read again later in her book *Faith Is Not a Feeling* . . .

One quiet summer day, Ney was meeting in the Colorado Rocky Mountains with 35 other women leaders from Campus Crusade. Suddenly sirens broke the peacefulness and megaphones barked, "Evacuate immediately! Evacuate immediately!" The group was told that the river was rising and floodwaters were rapidly approaching. The women immediately got into their cars and left. As they crossed over a bridge, they realized the urgency of the situation. The floodwaters washed away the bridge they had just driven over! Continuing on, the women traveled to a fork in the road, got out of their cars, asked for directions, jumped back into the cars, and drove on.

Ney Bailey's car went one way, and another car went a different way. Tragically, the seven women in the other car drowned. Not knowing of the deaths, though, Ney and her companions huddled together in prayer once their car reached higher ground. With the authority of Scripture undergirding her, she began, "Lord, Your Word says, 'In everything give thanks, because this is the will of God in Christ Jesus concerning us.' So while we are in this, we choose with our wills to thank You.

"And, Lord, Your Word says, 'All things'—including this—'work together for good to those who love You'—and we do—'and are called according to Your purpose'—and we are.

"You have also said that heaven and earth will pass away before Your Word passes away. So Your Word is truer than anything we are feeling or experiencing right now."[1]

As the title of Ney's book states, faith is not a feeling, and she lived out that truth in the situation described above. Despite whatever she was feeling—panic, fear, worry—she chose to put her faith in God and the truths of His Word and not in those feelings. As her prayer reveals, she turned to God and clung to the promises of His Word when her feelings and thoughts might have run wild.

And her prayer taught me three lessons I have tried to apply in my own Christian life. First, Ney showed me how to use the authority of Scripture in prayer. I saw right away the value of praying, "Your Word says . . ." and letting God's truths guide my petitions. Now, when-ever I counsel a woman who needs help praying about the difficult issues of her life, I give her a copy of Ney's prayer.

Second, Ney's prayer taught me how to use the truth of Romans 8:28 concerning my life. Following her model, now I pray, "God, Your Word says 'all things'—including this (and I name the present problem)—'work together for good.'" The simple exercise of filling in this blank forces me to acknowledge God's involvement in my life and reminds me that He is the source of my hope.

Third, this prayer taught me that I can never view my life through the lens of feelings. They are too varied and unstable. I must be faith oriented rather than feeling oriented, and, again, faith is not a feeling. Faith looks to God and trusts Him to work out the present difficulty for His purposes and my good. When I look to God and His Word—when I remember that He will indeed work all things for my good—I find hope.

As we saw in the preceding chapter, God is in complete control of every aspect of our life, and He promises to work "all things" for our good and His purposes. Now we'll look at three more reasons we can have hope in Him.

Trusting God's Good Purpose

In His promise of Romans 8:28, God reassures us that His purposes for us are good. The words are straightforward: "We know that God causes all things to work together for good." This truth that the end of all that He allows to touch our life will be good offers us hope for whatever life holds. God is working all things (as we've seen, no disclaimers or fine print here!) together for good. When we choose to believe that truth, we can't help but find hope in Him.

Again, we look to the Old Testament and see in Joseph a person who found hope in God despite the twists and turns his life took (Genesis 37–50). As the favored son of Jacob, Joseph found himself in great disfavor with his brothers. Acting out of hatred and envy, the brothers plotted Joseph's murder, but at the last moment they sold him into slavery instead. In Egypt, Joseph was slave to Potiphar, the captain of Pharaoh's bodyguard, and from here the enslaved Joseph—who remained faithful to God and was greatly blessed by Him—rose to a position of status within the Egyptian government. When famine struck Joseph's homeland, his brothers suddenly appeared before him in Egypt, asking for food to stay alive.

Joseph had a choice to make. He could fill his brothers' grain sacks with life-giving food, or he could have his brothers killed (either directly or, by withholding the grain, indirectly). As a man of God, Joseph extended grace to his brothers, saying, "As for you, you meant evil against me, but God meant it for good in order to bring about this present result, to preserve many people alive" (Genesis 50:20).

At this point in time—after being rejected, mistreated, sold into slavery, falsely accused, imprisoned, and forgotten—Joseph saw that God had been at work all along. Seeing God work all things for his family's good, Joseph found no reason to place blame and feel bitter. As Chuck Swindoll puts it, by choosing to see Jehovah at work, Joseph "blazes a new trail through a jungle of mistreatment, false accusations, undeserved punishment, and gross misunderstanding. He exemplifies forgiveness, freedom from bitterness, and an unbelievably positive attitude toward those who had done him harm."[2]

It's much too easy to let ourselves get bogged down in the tiny details of our own experience. Too often we spend a lot of time and energy sorting out how we feel, analyzing our emotions, deciding what we don't like, evaluating the pain, and choosing to worry, blame, or be angry. We may also try to figure out how we ourselves are going to make the situation better. This kind of introspection and focus on self hardly leads to hope. Instead of asking, "What does this mean to me?" asking

"What does this mean to God?" points us to the God of hope. We, like Joseph, can trust that God is working, and we can be women of hope knowing that the end is good because God is involved.

And the end is good because God Himself is good. In Matthew 7:9-10, Jesus asks, "What man is there among you, when his son shall ask him for a loaf, will give him a stone? Or if he shall ask for a fish, he will not give him a snake, will he?" Then Christ states a fact about God: "If you then, being evil, know how to give good gifts to your children, how much more shall your Father who is in heaven give what is good to those who ask Him!" (Matthew 7:11).

What God has given you may look and feel like a stone or a snake. But know that your heavenly Father, our good God, is working those things out for your good. A woman of hope looks at her life situation, at her powerful and redemptive God, and at the promises of Romans 8:28 and then chooses to believe that the end will be good, regardless of how life looks or feels in the present. By faith, she trusts God for the ultimate purpose He is working in her life.

The promise of Romans 8:28 serves as a lens through which we can have a godly perspective on our life, from birth to death. Because of these words, we can know that our good God is working the miracle of using the bad—everything from the most minor of incidents to the greatest of tragedies—for good. The fact that the end of all things will be good can give us hope and help us think beyond our present pain. After all, feelings distort our vision, and today's obstacles often prevent a hopeful view of the end. But by responding to God's love by loving Him and trusting in Him, we will be blessed with hope in His promise that He works all things for good.

Giving God Our Love

We can have hope in God because He works all things for our good and, as we'll see now, because we have given Him our love. Look again at Romans 8:28— "We know that God causes all things to work together for good *to those who love God . . .*" (emphasis mine). The words "to those who love God" are important because, as one scholar noted, the promise of Romans 8:28 "is not for everybody. It can be claimed only by those who love God."[3]

How do we show God our love for Him? Christ answered this question in nine words: "If you love Me, you will keep My commandments" (John 14:15). The Living Bible succinctly says, "If you love me, obey me." Our love for God is measured by our obedience.

Take a few minutes—now and regularly—to look at your life and evaluate how closely you are following God. When I do this, I take a pen and paper and run a check of my entire life. I ask myself, "Is there anything wrong in my relationship with God?" and I write down my answer. I then ask the same question regarding my husband, my children, my home, my personal growth, my areas of service to the Lord, and my relationships with other people. I write down everything that comes to my mind and then have a time of prayer, asking God's forgiveness for where I have been disobedient, unloving, and unfaithful. As 1 John 1:9 tells us, whenever we confess our sins like this, our good God "is faithful and righteous to forgive us our sins and to cleanse us from all unrighteousness."

You might choose to do this exercise during your regular prayer time. I encourage you to take some time each day to mentally examine the priority areas of your life—your relationship with God, your husband, and your children; how things are at home; your own spiritual growth; the challenges you face as you serve God;

the demands of the workplace; and your involvement with people. Look for areas where you have not obeyed God and His Word.

Because we demonstrate our love for God by obeying Him, it helps to begin each day by choosing to follow His ways all day long. My first-thing-in-the-morning prayer is that I will make His choice and do His will every minute and with every thought, word, and deed throughout the day. This prayer helps keep me alert to Him as I go about my day, meet people, do the tasks at hand, and face any challenges along the way.

And I pray this prayer again whenever the phone rings or I meet someone I know. I ask God to help me say the right words and do the right thing. If, for instance, the person who calls is upset, I pray, "Please, God, let me respond in Your way. . . . Help me stay calm. . . . Help me know when to speak and when to only listen. . . . Help me to help."

God works for good all things that happen to those who love Him, and we love God by obeying Him. And an evaluation of our current level of obedience gives us an idea of how warm our love for God is. Is your love red-hot and pure . . . lukewarm and indifferent . . . or ice-cold, below freezing? A pure and hot love for God can be a wellspring of hope in Him.

A God-Given Purpose

We can have hope in God because His purpose for us is good. We can have hope in God because we love Him and therefore the promise of Romans 8:28 is for us. To find yet another reason we can have hope in God, look once more at Romans 8:28 and note the closing words: "We know that God causes all things to work together for good to those who love God, *to those who are called according to His purpose*" (emphasis mine). Christians are "called ones"[4] in accordance with God's plan or purpose, and this calling was determined by God's sovereign, elective purpose.[5] And this calling gives significance as well as hope to our day-to-day existence.

I remember when my life had no purpose. As an average woman with an average marriage, two average preschool daughters, and an average house, I shook my fist at the kitchen ceiling one average and desperate day and cried, "There has to be more to life than this!" I was hopeless. After all, where could I find hope when I hadn't even found the purpose behind the things I was doing? My lack of purpose caused me to wonder, to doubt, and to rage, but God used my search for purpose to help me recognize that I needed Jesus Christ. Acting on that need, I became a Christian. Suddenly I saw the purpose of everything in my life because I saw that God had a purpose for me.

Knowing that God has a purpose for my life and my salvation brings great responsibility as well as great hope. I can no longer live my life according to my own desires, plans, or dreams: I exist totally for God's purposes. I am not to make decisions that will please people: I exist to serve God and His people according to the gifts He has blessed me with and in the situations He has placed me.

The constant awareness that God has a purpose for me personally has given me great hope when the day-to-day might otherwise weigh me down and leave me feeling as if I'm wandering in a maze in an English garden. These mazes, created by six- or seven-foot hedges, were used initially to provide some entertaining exercise for people after meals. The diners would enter the confusing and baffling network of shrubs and then try to find their way out.

As I've looked at pictures of these garden mazes, I've thought about how they are a metaphor for life. We move along in our Christian life, trying to serve God and follow His will, until we come to a corner which requires us to move in another direction. We then head in that new direction until the next turn where we're forced to go another way. We never know whom or what we'll encounter in the maze, and we don't know exactly where we're going. But we do know that, as we keep moving according to God's will and continue to go where He leads, He will fulfill His purpose in us. God doesn't ask us to understand the twists and the turns, the whys and the hows of life. He asks only that we trust that He is working His purpose in us as we live out our purpose of serving Him.

Knowing God's Will

Still, trying to determine God's will and specific purposes for us is not always easy. Acts 16:6-10 has taught me something about how God reveals His will to His people. In this passage, Luke (the writer of Acts) is reporting on Paul's second missionary journey. The apostle has been fulfilling God's purpose for his life by proclaiming the gospel. After preaching in one area of Asia Minor, he decided to travel in another direction but was "forbidden by the Holy Spirit to speak the word in Asia" (verse 6). With that direction blocked, Paul turned another way. Again, "the Spirit of Jesus did not permit them" (verse 7). Only one possibility remained, and Paul moved in that direction. When he did so, "a vision appeared to Paul in the night. . . . And when he had seen the vision, immediately we sought to go into Macedonia, concluding that God had called us to preach the gospel to them" (verses 9-10). Paul's response to God's leading in the maze of Asia Minor led to the birth of the church at Philippi.

When you, like Paul, seek to know God's will and be used for His ultimate purposes, He will guide you, as He did the apostle, through the maze of life. Although Luke does not say in Acts exactly how God forbade Paul to go in certain directions, the passage does teach us that we can trust God to close doors and block our path in order to keep us going where He wants us to go. Our role is to love God and keep moving through life according to His purpose for us. His role is to lead us in the maze so that we can fulfill the specific purposes He calls us to at the same time that He fulfills His purpose in and through us. And God uses people, events, and circumstances, both good and bad, to move us ultimately toward the fulfillment of His will for our life.

And, as Paul explains in Romans 8:29, the primary purpose of "all things" in our lives is Christlikeness: "For whom He foreknew, He also predestined to become conformed to the image of His Son." Everything—every person, every event—that touches our life is for the purpose of making us like Christ. We can find comfort and hope in the fact that God will use whatever He permits to happen to us to make us more like Jesus. Hear what minister and writer Alan Redpath says about the promise of Romans 8:28 and 29: "There is nothing—no circumstance, no trouble, no testing—that can ever touch me until, first of all it has gone past God and past Christ, right through to me. If it has come that far, it has come with a *great purpose*, which I may not understand at the moment. But as I *refuse* to become panicky, as I lift up my eyes to him and accept it as coming from the throne of God for some *great purpose of blessing* to my own heart, no sorrow will ever disturb me, no trial will ever disarm me, no circumstance will cause me to fret—for I *shall rest in the joy of what my Lord is*—That is the rest of victory."[6]

The truth of Romans 8:28 should indeed cause us to rest in the Lord and wait patiently for Him (Psalm 37:7)—for Him to act, for Him to work, for Him to save (if that is His will), for Him to reveal His purposes. Even if we never know why things happen, we can still rest in

God and hope in Him. In fact, we honor God when we choose to believe that He is loving, wise, and using every aspect of our life to make us more like Jesus.

Two women in particular have shown me how to live with hope in God. Striking examples of faith, these two women love God and trust His purposes for them despite tragedy, hardship, and suffering. May they encourage you to hope in the Lord.

Fanny Crosby

Fanny Crosby, the famous hymn writer, was a woman who believed that God's purposes are good and who clearly heard His calling on her life. Consider her comments about the doctor who unwittingly caused her blindness: "I have heard that this physician never ceased expressing his regret at the occurrence; and that it was one of the sorrows of his life. But if I could meet him now, I would say, 'Thank you, thank you, over and over again for making me blind.' . . . Although it may have been a blunder on the physician's part, it was no mistake on God's. I verily believe it was His intention that I should live my days in physical darkness, so as to be better prepared to sing His praises and incite others to do so."[7]

Through a doctor's apparent mistake, God gave to the church the wonderful songs of a blind Fanny Crosby who, with her increased spiritual insight, wrote hymns until she died at age 95, hymns which have endured and inspired others to greater faith.

When has someone else's blunder touched your life? When has someone else's mistake severely impacted you? A woman who hopes in God accepts unexplainable events as "no mistake on God's [part]." She knows that every event involves "His intention." A woman of hope looks to the God she loves for strength and lets His ability transform her disability.

Fanny Crosby found some of her options for life eliminated as she navigated the maze of her life, but—with God's blessing—she also discovered a uniquely personal way to serve Him and His people. Fanny Crosby couldn't see, but she could sing. She couldn't read, but she could write music. After the doctor's "mistake," she gave to God what she had—her singing and her writing—and He used her greatly for His kingdom.

Joni Eareckson Tada

When Joni Eareckson Tada was 17, she suffered a broken neck in a diving accident and was paralyzed from the neck down. As I write this, she is 43 years old. That's 26 years in her wheelchair, 26 years of physical therapy and surgeries, 26 years of nursing care. But, like Fanny Crosby, she gave to God what she had after the "accident"—her mind, her voice, her musical and artistic talents, her love for the Lord—and God is using her greatly.

If you've ever heard Joni speak, you know that Scripture flows out of her mouth. She has memorized Scripture from many translations, and God's own Word informs her words. And she has put many of those words on paper. She is the author of 17 books, with millions sold, many translated into several languages, and one addressing specifically the right to die issue (*When Is It Right to Die?*, published by Zondervan). She has also written the songs she sings and worked on a movie which tells her story of hope. She speaks at conferences, including Billy Graham Crusades and Moody Founders' Week, and her messages are shared over the radio and on tape. She also founded Joni and Friends, an organization which serves the handicapped.

Joni also uses her voice to serve the Lord and praise God. Instead of complaining and expressing self-pity,

Joni shares messages of hope, comfort, encouragement, and refreshment with millions of believers. Many of these messages come through songs which she herself sings and records despite the brace she wears. Her lovely voice is not the only way she uses her mouth to glorify God and offer hope to His people. Holding a brush in her teeth, Joni uses her mouth to paint, and her work has graced books and greeting cards. Again, Joni has given to God what she had left after the "accident"—her mind, her voice, her musical and artistic talents, her love for Him—and He is using her greatly for His kingdom.

Joni went through the maze of God's will and purpose. With her accident, she found many of her options in life eliminated, but God has opened up other options, blessed her in many ways, and enabled her to serve Him and His people around the world. Joni writes honestly of her struggles, but in her presence you witness a woman of hope, a woman who knows that God has promised to cause all things—including a tragic accident—to work together for her good and for His purpose. When I look at the life of Joni Eareckson Tada, I draw strength for my own.

Women of Hope

Ney Bailey, Fanny Crosby, and Joni Eareckson Tada. Each of these woman experienced tragedy in her life, and each of these women modeled hope in God despite that event—and you can do the same.

First, take inventory of your life. Chart the path you've walked. Review how God has shown you His will through the years. When did He stop you, turn you, send you back, or direct you in another way? How did God change your direction? Did He forbid something? Did He fail to permit something? Was there an "accident" or a "mistake" along the way, a tragedy, an unjust slander, an envious person, a failure, a lack, a handicap, an oversight, a deep hurt in your past?

Look again at the autobiography you have just sketched. Where has God worked bad for good? Where do you see Him making you more like Christ? If you have recognized God's unseen involvement along the way, you may now be able to pray as Ney Bailey taught us: "Lord, Your Word says 'All things—including this (fill in the blank)—work together for good to those who love You.'" You may even be able to thank God for His wisdom and ways, as unsearchable as they may sometimes be.

Perhaps your autobiography helps you see that it is in limiting that God reveals the limitlessness of His power and grace. In God's maze, "no" to one thing means "yes" to another. "No" in one direction is a clear indicator of "yes" in a different direction. "No" to certain pursuits means "yes" to others. With God as your guide, a "no" is never the end; a negative is never permanent. Even in the darkness that comes when we are unable to see how anything good could possibly come out of the bad, God's promise in Romans 8:28 offers us the light of hope. In fact, Romans 8:28 serves as a rainbow brilliantly and miraculously arching through the dark clouds that may hang over the maze of life, bringing the hope of God's promise that He works all things together for good for you who love Him.

10

Enduring Difficult Times

───────── ❧ ─────────

"For I know the plans that I have for you,"
declares the LORD . . .
Jeremiah 29:11

───────── ❧ ─────────

When my friend Judy moved from Missouri to California, she brought her country upbringing with her and began to create a country home for her family out West. During the fifteen years she has lived in her house, she has worked steadily on her dream of a country cottage.

When she was satisfied with the inside of her home, Judy went to work on her porch. There a cozy tea table and chairs are surrounded by a wooden bench, a bird cage, several birdhouses, baskets full of plants, and some gardening tools. A lounge chair, a wicker rocker, and a low table arranged around a braided rug invite you to relax. Tea on Judy's porch is indeed a special treat.

The porch complete, Judy began working on her garden. A walkway leads you from the porch to the left where wooden rails set off a U-shaped flower bed. There, flowering vines wrap around a trellis, the porch posts, and the rails. Stepping-stones take you to trimmed trees, and a bountiful Boston fern hangs from a low branch. Flowers have been carefully planted so that all the brilliant colors can be seen and enjoyed, and creeping figs

145

happily embrace the aged wooden fence. Judy's garden is a place of peace and beauty.

One evening, as our family visited with Judy's, my husband said, "Judy, this is a beautiful garden, but what happened over there?" Jim was pointing to the rock pile at the border of Judy's garden. Next to the rocks was a woodpile, a tree stump, a dead tree, some gravel, and an assortment of discarded flowerpots. The area spoke of barrenness and neglect.

But Judy said, "Oh, I have a plan!" and, glad to have an interested audience, grabbed a bulging manilla file folder. Spilling out of it were newspaper clippings, magazine articles, gardening tips, pictures of other gardens, instructions for choosing plants, and her drawings. For years, Judy had been collecting ideas and planning her ideal garden, and she was excited about her plan—"Oh, I have a plan!"

God's Plans

"Oh, I have a plan" is exactly what God is telling the Israelites in Jeremiah 29:11. To the children of Israel who have been uprooted from their homes and carried away as captives to Babylon—and to you and me as well—God declares, "I know the plans that I have for you . . . plans for welfare and not for calamity to give you a future and a hope."

Although the heartbroken prophet Jeremiah prophesied doom for these stiff-necked people who had turned away from God, he also preached hope to these captives, hope that was based on this promise God made to them. Having announced their sentence of seventy years of bondage in Babylon, Jeremiah then told these displaced Jews how to survive those years, and his words can help us when we, like the Israelites, find ourselves in places or predicaments we didn't choose for ourselves.

According to Jeremiah, we need to first recognize God's hand in what has happened. Speaking through Jeremiah, God twice told the Israelites, "I have sent you into exile" (29:4,7). God explained to them that it wasn't the Babylonians alone who had taken them away from their homeland. God Himself had allowed it. Likewise, whatever circumstances you and I find ourselves in, we need to remember that God has allowed us to be there. The situation may not be our ideal, but it is in God's hands. Your life is not out of control. Nothing just randomly happened to get you where you don't want to be. We find peace when we acknowledge that God is indeed in control of our circumstances.

Having acknowledged God's control of our life, we are then to—as we've looked at before—bloom where we are planted. We are to go on loving the Lord and fulfilling His purposes for us wherever we find ourselves and no matter how undesirable or unexpected the circumstances. Jeremiah told those crushed and bewildered people of Israel how to live during their exile: "Build houses and live in them; and plant gardens, and eat their produce. Take wives and become the fathers of sons and daughters, and take wives for your sons and give your daughters to husbands, that they may bear sons and daughters; and multiply there and do not decrease" (29:5,6). The priorities of marriage, family, and home life were to be their focus—not their pain. God called them to make a home, plant crops, and bear fruit in the land of their affliction. Life was to go on for them, and it is to go on for you and me. Whatever sorrow or situation we may be facing, God wants us to continue building our home.

After giving specific instructions to the Israelites, Jeremiah then pronounced God's promise of a return to their homeland and these words: "For I know the plans that I have for you . . . plans for welfare and not for calamity to give you a future and a hope." Whenever these misplaced people were discouraged, they were to find their security and hope in God and this promise—and so are we. The plans God has for us are indeed a source of real security, no matter what challenges, hurts, and questions we face along the way.

Unshakable Security

Loving God with all our mind means getting to know Him better, and when we know God—His love, His power, His wisdom, His goodness—we can be secure about today and tomorrow. After all, we know that God has promised to work all things for our good and His purposes (Romans 8:28), no matter what the present circumstances might lead us to feel and believe. We know that, despite the rocky path we may now be walking, God is at work for our ultimate good and the fulfillment of His good purposes. We find an anchor for the future in God's promise that He has a plan and purpose for our life. We find security in God.

When we find security in the God we know and love, we also see with eyes of faith beyond the sorrow and suffering we are experiencing. We see the Father who never forgets His child, His plan, or His promise of future good, and that vision can sustain us through the growing pains of God's maturing and pruning process in our life. Instead of giving in to the pain that often comes with growth, we look to God, His truth, and His promises. Again, we find security in Him.

When we don't look to God and the truths of His Word, insecurity results. If our thoughts are not in line with what the Bible teaches, we are thinking lies, and those untrue thoughts will feed our fantasies and fears. We will too easily focus on the past or the future rather than on the present reality, and thinking about the unreal past and future leads to uncertainty and even panic.

Remembering your gracious God and His promise of good plans for you and focusing your thoughts on His purposes for your life can counter such uncertainty and insecurity. Panic, despair, nervousness, bewilderment, fear—God speaks against emotions like these in His Word. In fact, when the circumstances of life might lead to uncertainty and confusion, the promise of Jeremiah 29:11 gives us certainty and hope: God has a plan for our welfare. The path of life may zig and zag, twist and turn, but God has promised you and me "a future and a hope." With that promise as a lens through which to look at life, we don't need to know the future. Instead, we can be content and at peace knowing the Father, whose plans are for good and not evil. All will be well. We can be secure in that fact and we can therefore endure to the end of the bondage and build and bear fruit in the meantime.

Free to Serve

The security we find in God's promised plan for us frees us to serve Him wherever we are. Although we can never know the full scope of God's will for our lives, we do know that He calls us to serve Him and His people (Matthew 20:26-28). When we know that God's plan for our future is one of goodness and hope, we can trust that to God and concentrate on serving Him in the present.

In fact, this is the message Jeremiah delivered to the captive Israelites who, as one commentator observed, "are having their first taste of the bitterness of exile."[1] As we've seen, Jeremiah was specific about how the Israelites were to endure their hard years of exile: "The captives in Babylon were to settle down and live as normally as possible under the circumstances (build houses, marry, multiply . . . and pray)."[2] In other words, the children of Israel were to serve God in their marriages, their families, their community, and their businesses.

That is our assignment, too. If we are married, God calls us to serve our husband. A Christian wife is on assignment from God to help her husband (Genesis 2:18) and to nurture and love her children (Titus 2:4)—wherever she is. To fulfill these roles properly requires energy, self-sacrifice, and the strength and grace which God alone provides. Each of us—married or single—is also called to serve the body of Christ, His church (1 Corinthians 12:7). Wherever we are and whatever our circumstances, we are to serve God.

God's Servants

When we look to the Bible as well as to believers who have gone before us, we find rich and inspiring examples of people who served God wholeheartedly. Look again, for instance, at Joseph's life. He served God as a slave, as a prisoner, and finally as an official in the Egyptian government. He served God as the trusted manager of Potiphar's luxurious palace as well as from a dark, dank dungeon where he was in irons and his feet were fastened with fetters (Psalm 105:18). Finally released from prison after three years of unjust punishment, Joseph became second in command in Egypt, and his service extended beyond that country's boundaries to the entire known world as he dispensed life-giving grain during a serious famine. Joseph served, no matter where he was, no matter what his situation, and no matter who needed his service.

The apostle Paul also models service to us. Whether he was standing on the heights of Mars Hill debating with the best minds from the highest court of Athens or chained to a single guard in the depths of a dungeon, he served his Lord as a preacher of the gospel. And, despite beatings, stonings, death threats, imprisonments, and various other forms of suffering, Paul kept on preaching (see 2 Corinthians 11:23-33).

In the eighteenth century, we find the example of Jeanne Marie Guyon. Imprisoned in the Bastille (described by some as the most horrible prison on earth), Madame Guyon spent four of her seven years there in solitary confinement. While serving her sentence, she focused her thoughts on God. The result of her time and meditation was her writing. She wrote many books, including a twenty-volume commentary on the Bible.[3]

In more recent times, Mrs. C. T. Studd also models for us service in every circumstance. She served her missionary husband as his wife and, while she was healthy, as his manager. As she grew increasingly ill and even as an invalid, Mrs. Studd continued to serve God. One biographer writes, "She had to go to her room each night at seven and not come down the next day till lunch time. . . . From her bed and invalid couch she formed Prayer Centres, issued monthly pamphlets by the thousand, wrote often twenty to thirty letters a day, planned and edited the first issues of the *Heart of Africa Mission Magazine*."[4] Mrs. Studd served in sickness as well as in health.

Hudson Taylor also served God wherever he was. When illness forced him to leave his ministry in China and return to England, he used this "downtime" to found the China Inland Mission. When he returned to China, he had created a mission organization to support him and had recruited new missionaries to accompany him.[5]

I am also blessed to have a close personal friend exemplify service to God in every situation. Suzy has lived with the Epstein-Barr virus for fifteen years. From her sickbed in her darkened bedroom, however, Suzy serves God and His people. For one thing, she has time to talk on the phone and offer counsel and encouragement to the young wives and mothers who call for advice and friendship. Other women are too busy for such lengthy conversations. In accordance with the instruction of Titus 2:3-5, Suzy offers herself, her gifts, and her wisdom to younger women in the body of Christ, and she does so despite her limited lifestyle.

Like all these examples I've mentioned—and countless others I could list—you and I can serve God no matter what our circumstances. He calls us to serve Him and, through the prophet Jeremiah's words to suffering captives, He calls us to serve Him even when we're not where we want to be and when life is not easy. Despite their Babylonian exile, the children of Israel were to keep living for God, serving Him, and praying. As one Bible editor observes, "Life cannot grind to a halt during troubled times. In an unpleasant or distressing situation, we must adjust and keep moving. . . . When you enter times of trouble or sudden change, pray diligently and move ahead, doing whatever you can rather than giving up because of uncertainty."[6] Put simply, we are to serve God—no matter what.

Delighting in the Lord

God's plan for you involves serving Him at all times, in all places, and in all situations, and such service is to grow naturally out of our love for our heavenly Father. Nurturing our relationship to God enables us to walk more closely to Him through our days, and that closeness gives us greater sensitivity to Him and what His plans for us would be. In fact, consider the truth of Psalm 37:4—"Delight yourself in the LORD; and He will give you the desires of your heart." When we walk closely to God and delight in Him, He puts into our heart the desires we find there. Consequently, our plans agree with His plans because they *are* His plans.

Let's first look at the beginning of Psalm 37:4. To delight yourself in the Lord means to seek your pleasure in Him, to make Him your true joy.[7] In fact, the Septuagint reads, "Indulge thyself in the Lord."[8] Delighting yourself in the Lord also suggests that you are loving God with your whole being. God, His Word, and His ways are the focus and foundation of your life, and He is what matters most to you.

Again, if you delight in God, He will put His desires into your heart. His desires will be your desires, and your desires will be His. You won't know where one leaves off and the other begins because you will be delighting in Him to the point that you are adopting His thoughts and His ways. His plans are becoming your plans and your plans are becoming His.

Reading God's Word

Have you ever noticed that the more you are with someone, the more you become like that person? That is what Christian discipleship and walking with God are all about. Perhaps you've noticed that you and your husband use the same figures of speech and share many of the same opinions and perspectives on life. Perhaps you've been surprised to see your child reflect your attitudes and mannerisms. The more we are with someone, the more we can become like that person. This same principle holds true when it comes to spending time with God by studying His Word. The more time you spend reading the Bible, the more you will resemble God. You will begin to think as God thinks, which leads to Christlike behavior, and you will begin to desire what He desires.

The Navigators teach "God's Word, the first word," an exhortation to put the Bible before other things. For me, that means not turning on the television or radio and not reading the newspaper before I spend some time reading the Bible. When I start my day with God's Word and get in tune with His perspective, I find myself walking more closely with Him through the day and delighting in Him more wholeheartedly. Also, when I do hear the news or read the paper, I am already thinking God's thoughts and can filter what I hear through His Word. Delighting myself in the Lord means, for me, attempting each day to choose Him, and that means choosing to make more time for His Word than any other kind of input.

I encourage you to take a moment to consider the kind of input which may be influencing your attitudes, expectations, and approach to life. If we're spending five minutes with the Bible and five hours with the television talk shows and soap operas, our values, our standards, and our views on life, marriage, and the world may not be God's. We may instead be thinking the way the world thinks and, consciously or unconsciously, responding the way the people on those programs respond.

Lining up our thoughts with God's thoughts comes when we spend time with Him and learn what His thoughts are. If you delight yourself in the Lord and spend time reading His Word, you will know His thoughts. As you spend more time with God, He will work in your heart and your mind to make you more like Him. Furthermore, He will give you the desires of your heart, which will be the desires of His heart.

Committing Ourselves to the Lord

Delighting in the Lord, knowing His Word, and, third, committing ourselves to the Lord are ways to ensure that our plans for us match God's plans for us. Psalm 37:5 says, "Commit your way to the LORD, trust also in Him, and He will do it." As one commentator explains, committing yourself and your activities to the Lord "involves the committal of the life. [This is] utter trust [and] abandonment of the whole life in simple and unreserved faith to God Almighty. . . . [When we do so,] He will act. He will bring [that which matters most in any life] to pass."[9] A paraphrase of this promise could read, "Trust God to take over your career, home, work, all the circumstances, aims and ambitions of life, and He will so mould events that your deepest and purest desires shall find unmeasured fulfillment and life will be filled with utter satisfaction."[10] What a promise! What hope! What a plan God has for us, His children!

Like Psalm 37:5, Proverbs 16:3 offers us a command and a promise: "Commit your works to the LORD, and your plans will be established." The New International Version reads, "Commit to the Lord whatever you do, and your plans will succeed." In other words, you and I will find our thoughts, plans, and activities established and blessed when we commit to God every aspect of our life, and we can experience this wonderful truth each day. When in prayer we commit the day to God and dedicate it to Him, He can direct our thoughts, plans, dreams, and acts for the rest of the day.

When I dedicate the day to God, I find myself being a better steward of the minutes and hours. I am more sensitive to His presence and therefore to how He would have me serve Him and be a witness for Him. In practical terms, dedicating my day to God doesn't fit with yelling at the children, nursing worry or depression, overeating, or wasting time. I won't want to do such things during a day I have committed to God. I want my plans to be His plans for me and His plans to be mine as I go through the day.

Delighting in the Lord, reading His Word, and committing ourselves to Him are indeed ways we can love God each day. These ways of loving God also enable us to serve Him better because they bring us closer to Him. And serving God—no matter what has happened or is happening—is part of His plan for us. Regardless of where you and I have been placed by God, we can bloom and bear fruit there. After all, just as Judy was able to say about her garden, "Oh, I have a plan," God is able to say about your life and mine, "Oh, I have a plan!" What comfort and assurance, what hope and what security there is in the thought that God has a plan for us!

11

Becoming God's Masterpiece

───────── ❧ ─────────

"For I know the plans that I have for you,"
declares the LORD,
"plans for welfare and not for calamity
to give you a future and a hope."
Jeremiah 29:11

───────── ❧ ─────────

J ust as my friend Judy had a plan and a design for her garden, God has a plan for your life. Regardless of how your life may look or feel right this moment, know that God is busy at work on His plan for you. Remember, too, that His plan reflects His purposes, His methods, and His timetable. As we've seen, God's timetable for the Israelites involved seventy years of captivity in Babylon (Jeremiah 29:10). That seventy years was a death sentence for those who heard the prophet's words. They would die without ever seeing Jerusalem again. God's promise of peace and restoration would be fulfilled for a future generation.

Imagine learning God's pronouncement that you would never again see your homeland. It might be easy to feel that God is turning His back on you, that He no longer loves you, and that He is no longer merciful or just—and all these would be incorrect thoughts. To prevent such wrong thinking, God gives the Israelites—right on the heels of the seventy-year sentence—the promise we've been looking at: "For I know the plans that I have for you," declares the LORD, "plans for welfare and not for calamity to give you a future and a hope" (Jeremiah 29:11).

As the children of Israel sorrowed and suffered in Babylon for seventy years, they would find security only in God and His promise, and the same is true for you and me. We find hope in a hostile place when we focus on the goodness of God as revealed in His promises. In other words, hope and security come when we—like the Israelites—acknowledge God's love for us. The people in exile would have to take God at His word and realize that He would not forget them and that He would restore them to peace and prosperity. For seventy years they would have to place their faith, hope, and trust in these words of assurance spoken to them by God through a prophet. We've seen already one reason why those words of Jeremiah offer all the security God's people, then and now, need. First of all, God has a plan for you, one aspect of which is to serve Him because you love Him. Let's look again at Jeremiah 29:11 for other reasons we can find security in the promise God makes there.

God's Good Plan: An Adventure

When my husband said, "Judy, this is a beautiful garden, but what happened over there?" Judy replied, "Oh, I have a plan!" Of course Judy's plan was for beauty, order, and growth. She would never plan an ugly garden or a garden that couldn't flourish. Likewise, God would never plan for you a life of ugliness, a life where you couldn't flourish in Him. This truth can indeed offer us security, and keeping this thought in mind can give us hope whatever challenges and difficulties we currently face.

If the circumstances of your life seem overwhelming right now and the fulfillment of God's promise far removed, try thinking about God's plan as an adventure. This perspective can change your attitude as you realize that you are in something of a secret conspiracy with the Creator of the universe and the Author of your life. Know that His plan will end in good for you, rest secure in that truth, and relax in Him despite the ups and downs, the twists and turns of the path that will eventually get you there. Let your life be your personal adventure with God.

The attitude that life is an adventure greatly helped my friend Lauren and her mother deal with the events of their trip to Southern California a few years ago. Coming down from Seattle to visit Lauren's sister in San Diego before attending the women's retreat at our church, they were already in San Diego when the Rodney King verdict was announced and rioting began in Los Angeles. The violence closed down businesses and freeways and led our church elders to close the church campus and cancel the retreat.

When Sunday morning arrived, however, the city was calm and Lauren decided that she would drive up to attend worship services at our church. After putting on their church dresses, she and her mother started north. Somewhere along the way, they missed a freeway exit, got lost, and never made it to church. They decided to visit a friend near Los Angeles so that they could attend the evening service. When I saw them that night, I learned that they would be staying in L.A. overnight, so I asked them to come for brunch the next morning.

Early Monday I drove out to their friend's home to lead them through the freeway traffic to my house so they wouldn't get lost again. When they opened the front door, though, they still had their Sunday best on— the only clothes they'd taken from San Diego!

After a wonderful visit with them, I walked them out to their car and hugged them goodbye. As they drove away, however, I realized I hadn't given Lauren directions to the freeway. We live within one mile of six freeways, and none of them has an on-ramp for San Diego. They would be lost again—and indeed they were, as I learned weeks later. But Lauren and her mother laughed as we talked. Nothing had bothered them because they were on an adventure.

Their trip to Los Angeles had been one disaster and disappointment after another. No retreat, no refund, no Sunday morning worship, no directions, and no clothes—and lost in L.A. twice! But their trust in their good God, whose plans are good and not evil, let them approach each event as part of an amazing adventure. They didn't seem to feel as angry and frustrated as I tend to feel when things don't fit with my schedule or go as planned. They didn't complain, gripe, or get upset, as I also tend to do. Focusing on the fact that God has a plan for your good will make you secure and adventuresome instead of just disappointed and frustrated. Jeremiah 29:11 invites us to accept the Christian life as an adventure and ride the roller coaster of life, knowing that God's plan is for our good.

God's Good Plan: A Process

One reason many of us fail to enjoy the adventure of the Christian life is the fact that it is a process. We like end results more than we like the process that gets us there. But between today and the good end which God promises, we have to go through a process. Like the Israelites, we have to experience the blows before we can experience the blessings, a truth which comes to life for me in the following illustration.

I remember hearing the following story from Michelangelo's life, a story which gave me an important image for what God is doing in my life and yours. One day a colossal cube of marble was delivered to the artist's studio. Michelangelo walked around it several times, surveying it from a step back and then looking at it closely. He touched it with his hands and even pressed his face against the cold block of stone. Suddenly he grabbed a mallet and a chisel and swung mightily. Blow after blow caused small chips of marble as well as large chunks to fly in every direction.

Watching in awe, his apprentice screamed above the noise of shattering stone, "What are you doing? You are ruining a perfect piece of marble!"

With the passion of an artist with a vision, Michelangelo answered, "I see an angel in there, and I've got to get him out!"

God looks at you with the same kind of eyes Michelangelo looked at the piece of marble and says, "I see an angel in there, and I've got to get her out!" God sees in you an "angel." He sees in you the image of Christ and wants to set that free. The process of life is the process of freeing that "angel." In the words of Jeremiah, the process of life involves plans for good and "not of evil, to give you an expected end" (29:11 KJV).

From time to time, you and I may—like Michelangelo's apprentice—cry out in bewilderment and terror, "What are you doing? You are ruining a perfect piece of marble!" Such a cry reveals our failure to understand the Artist, His vision, and the process of His work. God picks up His hammer and chisel and, acting out of His infinite love and wisdom, starts chipping away at the piece of marble that is our life. He carefully knocks off the unimportant, the meaningless, and the excess. His chisel cuts away the flaws and removes all that is ugly. He wants to make us Christlike and perfect. He wants to make us His masterpiece. While at times the process may be puzzling and even painful, we can be secure in the knowledge that it is for good, not evil.

For a perspective on these puzzling and painful times, however, consider another example from the world of art. To give depth to a painting, Old World artists would first wash their white canvas with black. Only by beginning with that black could they later achieve the contrast, color, dimension, and depth they desired. After all, no painting is a masterpiece that possesses only one color or one intensity. When the canvas of our life seems to be washed with black, we can remember the promise of Jeremiah 29:11 that the end will be good. We can let God's Word enable us to stand secure in the hope that, when God completes His good plans, our life will have greater depth, a more interesting dimension, and remarkable intensity. The Artist is at work giving us a Christlike character. The Artist is making a masterpiece.

God's Good Plan: An Opportunity

The adventure of life is often difficult, and God's process in your life may be quite painful at times. I have found it helpful to try to profit from every single experience that comes my way, the difficult and painful times as well as those times when life is going smoothly. In her book *What Is a Family?* Edith Schaeffer advises that we treat adversity as an opportunity. She encourages us to regard hard times as important to our spiritual and personal growth, not merely something we have to endure. She challenges us to make adversity count for something positive by learning all we can from it. And these words do not come glibly. Mrs. Schaeffer knows pain and adversity.

Hear her words—those of a mother whose daughter suffered for two years with rheumatic fever and whose son was born with polio:

> For my own children I always tried to remind them to take the opportunity to get

all the information and interesting facts they
could, in the midst of their own times
in hospitals or dentists' chairs! "You may
never have this chance again; find out all
you can." Not only does it help to alleviate
the fears and take minds off pain, but it is an
honest fact that one may never have another
chance to see certain things and to ask certain questions. "Now is your chance to find
out all you can about a . . . hospital."—"Now
is your chance to see how a blood transfu-
sion works."—"Now you can read on that
bottle what is mixed in the liquid they are
about to put into you instead of food."—
"See if you can look at the X ray of that leg.
Amazing the way a bone is apart!"[1]

Edith Schaeffer is hardly encouraging us to down-
play or look away from the hard times of life and the pain
those times bring. Instead, she is saying to look right in
the face of adversity and learn from it. It's an opportunity from God to learn something we might not learn
otherwise, and it's an opportunity that God is using for
our good.

God's Good Plan: A Fact

Thinking of God's plan for our life as an adventure, a
process, and an opportunity can improve our attitude
when the hard times come, the question marks loom,
and the pain overwhelms. Furthermore, realizing as well
that God's plan for good is fact—unshakable truth—can
give us a sense of security when life seems anything but
secure. A pastor at our church understood this clearly
and let this truth shape his approach to problem-solving
and giving counsel.

Whenever someone approached Jerry with whatever difficulty was at hand, he put a note in a file folder he had labeled "Wait a Week." During that week, Jerry prayed over every situation he had filed. At the end of that week of prayer, he pulled out each paper and prayed, "Okay, Lord, what are we going to do?"

What amazed me most about this entire procedure was Jerry's attitude. His full counseling schedule meant he heard about a lot of heartache, but it in no way affected his personality or his outlook on life. Whenever we saw Jerry, he greeted us with a smile, a lot of energy, and the statement, "God is still on His throne." Clearly, Jerry was secure in God's promises.

You and I can be just as secure in God's promises as Jerry was. God has a plan for us that will be good, and the truth that He is still on His throne means that nothing can interfere with His plans. The truth of God's love, power, and faithfulness can offer security even when our feelings overwhelm. From our perspective, a situation may look hopeless. From the throne of God, however, the situation is part of the process that is making us more Christlike and moving us closer to the fulfillment of the good plans God has for us.

God's Good Plan: Purging and Pruning

When my husband said, "Judy, this is a beautiful garden, but what happened over there?" he was pointing to an area that was not beautiful at all. He was pointing to the rocks that would have to be carted off; the rotten pieces of fence that would have to be replaced; the dead tree that would have to be removed; the tree stump that would have to be ground into chips; the sick shrubs that would have to be dug out; and the packed earth that would have to be rototilled before it could sustain any plant life. Everything in that part of the yard that was ugly, old, dead, diseased, and useless would have to be eliminated and destroyed before Judy could complete her beautiful garden, and that cleanup was part of her plan.

God works the same way in our life. Before His plan can come to full fruition in our life, He must eliminate all that is old, dead, diseased, and useless in our character. When we first meet Sarah in the Old Testament, for instance, she is impatient, contentious, angry, manipulative, and unbelieving. Her life with Abraham, Hagar, and Ishmael is characterized by tension and unfulfillment. But God works in her life and uses failures, consequences, time, and even unhappiness to bring her to a mature faith in Him. In fact, she is listed in Hebrews 11 as an example of faith. While such a pruning process as Sarah underwent can be painful, it gives us an opportunity to love God by trusting that He is at work in our life to bring about the beauty He has promised.

The Nature of God

God's promises do indeed offer us security, but only if we know that God is trustworthy and good. Promises mean little when made by someone who is evil and therefore untrustworthy. We must therefore establish in our mind that God can only think and do good or, put in opposite terms, God cannot think or do evil. After all, our thoughts influence our behavior.

If, for instance, you believe that God can think evil thoughts and do evil deeds, you will never be secure. Instead, you will suspect that evil and harm are around every corner. If, however, you govern your thoughts by the truth that God cannot think or do evil, you can proceed through each day of your life secure in God's love for you and confident in the knowledge that God's goal for you is good. This security brings peace, hope, and joy.

To keep my thoughts in line with the truth that God cannot think or do evil, I rely on my collection of "goodness verses." I let passages like Psalm 34:8,10, Psalm 107:8,9, Psalm 84:11, Romans 8:28, James 1:17, and Nahum 1:7 guide my prayers whenever I need to remember that I am secure in God. Such verses have helped me as well as the women who have come to me for counsel.

Gayle came to me when the circumstances of her life gave her reason to wonder about God and His goodness, so I encouraged her to memorize one of my "goodness verses" each week. Once she memorized these words of truth and hope, God could use them to offer her comfort, and I could refer to them to remind her of God's goodness and the security we can have in Him.

I also had her write out a prayer using the verses. Every time she thought about her situation or had to face the people involved, she could read her prayer and again remind herself of the truth about God. As she felt anger, sadness, and discouragement, she could turn to the prayer and remember that God is good and that His plan for her is good.

Here is Gayle's prayer of assurance: "Father God, I want to thank You for Your sovereign power in my life, that You arrange all circumstances—past, present and future—for good for me because I love You and am called according to Your purposes (Romans 8:28). It gives me great assurance and security in You to know that You know the plans You have for me regarding *(situation, person, problem),* and I can rest in the fact that You want only the best for me, a future and a hope (Jeremiah 29:11). Help me to remember that Your provision is all encompassing. You are the Giver and the Protector. You will withhold no good thing from me if I walk uprightly in Your will (Psalm 84:11). Please teach me to fear You [and reverence You], Lord, and to really know what that means, for then I will have no want (Psalm 34:9)."

Writing your own prayer and incorporating your own "goodness verses" in it will help you view the challenges and hurts of your life through the lens of Scripture's truth. As you draw closer to God in prayer, focus on the fact of His goodness, consider His power, and meditate on His promises, He will bless you with His peace and a sense of security in His love. God has plans for you and His plans are for good because God Himself is good. He can neither think nor do evil.

The Fulfillment of the Promise

Have you ever planned a vacation to mark the end of a long project or a special evening out to celebrate the completion of a difficult task? Rewards like these are effective motivators. We can endure hard times as long as we know there is something good at the end. We can work hard and sacrifice meals, sleep, and fun when the goal and the reward are worthwhile.

God knew that the seventy-year exile would be difficult, so when He pronounced that sentence He also promised the Israelites a reward—an expected end, a future and a hope, and the restoration of peace and prosperity.[2] As one commentator observed, God did not want "that unexpectant apathy which is the terrible accompaniment of so much worldly sorrow . . . to be an ingredient in the lot of the Jews."[3] The promise He held out—the promise that they would have an end, "literally, an 'end and expectation' meaning such an end as they wished for"[4]—offered them security, hope, and a reason to persevere.

God knows, too, that your life and mine will be difficult, so He has given us the Book of Revelation. This ultimate fulfillment of God's promises and purposes will indeed be glorious as His victory over Satan is made complete. This future will also be right and good because, by nature, God is right and good. This promise of

God's planned and perfect future ministers to me in three different ways.

First, God's promise rebukes me when I am tempted to doubt God and question His management of my life. I can almost hear God chiding, "Wait a minute! The plans I have for you are for good and not for evil, and I will indeed bring that good about. I *will* bring you to an expected end." Although I do not know the specifics of this promised end or what God will do in my life and my character to get me where He wants me to be, I can trust in the fact that He knows.

Besides offering rebuke, God's promise gives me comfort. He uses Jeremiah 29:11 to calm my emotions. Through the prophet's words, God whispers, "It's okay. You don't have to worry. You don't have to wonder about anything. I know the plans I have for you, and they are plans for good and not for evil. I'll bring you to the expected end." God uses this verse to remind me that He has complete knowledge of my life, a plan for me that is for good, and the ability to make that plan happen. With that reminder, God gives me the peace that comes with security in Him.

Jeremiah 29:11 offers rebuke, comfort, and, finally, encouragement. Through the promise in that verse, God encourages me when I am tempted to despair. He prods, "Keep going! Don't give up your hope! And don't worry about the end! The plans I have for you are plans for good and not for evil, to bring you to an expected end." Through this promise, God reminds me that, no matter how hard or long the journey, I am going to get to the end and the end is going to be good. And—I've saved the best for last—God's greatest promise for His children is heaven. Heaven is the expected end for all who name Jesus as Lord and Savior. Ultimately, the final future and hope for us who are God's children is heaven, where there will be fullness of joy and pleasures forevermore at His right hand (Psalm 16:11).

Living Out the Promise

Jeremiah 29:11 assures us that God's plans for us personally and for His people in general are for good, not evil. When you and I meditate on truths like this one, we are responding to God's love for us by trusting Him. We are also able to find security for any and every situation we'll encounter in life—birth, death, marriage, singleness, widowhood, poverty, persecution, the unknown of a move, or the permanence of being in an unpleasant place. God's promise leaves no phase or issue of life uncovered. And I am always encouraged when I see someone living out her trust in God and this wonderful promise.

Just this morning, for example, a pastor's wife called to tell me that her husband was resigning from his church. Margo reported, "Liz, I've been reciting Jeremiah 29:11 all day long. I know God was involved in bringing us here. I know we have learned many lessons and been used in many ways. I also know God has a plan for us and that it is a good plan, not evil. He will bring us to an expected end. He knows where we are going."

These are the thoughts of a woman who is secure in her knowledge that God is good and that His plans for her and her husband are good as well. In the midst of all that she is feeling now that her life has been turned upside down, Margo is using her mind to focus on the truths of Scripture. Margo is dealing with fear, disappointment, worry, anger, confusion, and hurt as she anticipates saying goodbye, being uprooted from her home, and moving in an unknown direction to an unknown place, but she is nevertheless confident in God's perfect plan. The foundations of her daily life have suddenly collapsed and the security of their income has slipped away, but Margo knows God, His goodness, and His promises. She is enjoying victory in her thought life as she brings each thought into captivity to the truth of

Jeremiah 29:11. In the eye of the hurricanes which come our way in life, you and I—like Margo—can find unshakable security in our loving God who promises us that His plans for us are for good, not evil.

12

Majoring on the Minors

Oh, the depth of the riches
both of the wisdom and knowledge of God!
Romans 11:33

————— ❧ —————

During my years as a Christian, I have been blessed to know some fine Christian women who have modeled for me faith in God and service to Him. One of these very special women is Sarah Coleman, whom I first got to know about fifteen years ago when her husband became our church's choir director. Sarah has spoken around the world on missions, Christian education, singleness, and management. She has written six books, started several successful companies, and founded the Christian service organization InterCristo. She is on the board of directors for several Christian organizations, and, before she was married at age 47, Sarah had planned to retire at age 50 and serve on the mission field, fully self-supported.

An amazing woman who inspires everyone she meets, Sarah has indeed inspired me. Her wisdom, her love for God, and her commitment to memorizing Scripture have helped shape my ministry and message. I vividly remember, for instance, talking with her at a holiday party ten years after she had moved on from our church. During the chance we had to catch up, I asked her a question, and her answer has changed my life. "Sarah," I said, "if you were to write another book for women, what would it be about?"

She said, "Liz, I don't like what I see when I go into Christian bookstores. There are so few books for women about God. If I were to write a new book to share with women what I have learned through the years, I would call it *Forever Father*. Women today have so many problems simply because they don't know God. We are majoring on the minors."

"Majoring on the minors"—I have literally spent hours thinking about these words. Sarah's observation changed my philosophy of ministry, my studies, the books I choose to read, the way I use my time, and the ideas I share with other women. Her observation also explains to me why she is such a powerful model of faith. Throughout her life, Sarah has majored on knowing God. As a result, she possesses clear vision, a sound mind, and the wisdom to know what really counts in the Christian life.

And what really counts in the Christian life is knowing God because that knowledge is foundational if we are to live for Him, truly love Him, and joyfully serve Him. It is, however, much easier to major on the minors than on the Person of God. We tend, for instance, to focus on our problems rather than on our all-loving and all-powerful God. We tend to focus on our troubles rather than on our trustworthy, faithful Lord. We tend to look at the entangling evils of the world around us rather than to our God's holy and heavenly majesty. And, sadly, we in the formal ministry of the church too often focus on meeting needs, providing support, and facilitating fellowship rather than on the God whose church we are.

As a young believer, however, I had the blessed opportunity to major on God as I met with small groups of women to study A. W. Tozer's *The Knowledge of the*

Holy, J. B. Phillips' *Your God Is Too Small*, and J. I. Packer's *Knowing God*. As these book titles suggest, the classes focused on the Person and character of God. As we got to know God better, we found ourselves truly in awe of Him, and we found ourselves growing in our walk with Him. We were majoring on what mattered and found ourselves richly blessed.

And that is not surprising. As A. W. Tozer writes, "A right conception of God is basic not only to systematic theology but to practical Christian living as well. . . . I believe there is scarcely an error in doctrine or a failure in applying Christian ethics that cannot be traced finally to imperfect and ignoble thoughts about God."[1] Like Sarah, Tozer calls us to know God, and knowing God comes with knowing His Word. When we know our heavenly Father and trust in His Word, we can lead a life that glorifies and honors Him. And as we grow to love God more completely—with our mind as well as our heart—we can say, with Paul, "Oh, the depth of the riches both of the wisdom and knowledge of God! How unsearchable are His judgments and unfathomable His ways!" (Romans 11:33). As we come to know God better, we will also find it easier to know, follow, and accept His will for our life.

Acknowledging the Wisdom of God

When we know God and recognize fully His deep love for us, we will more willingly and freely yield ourselves to His plan for us and our life. Although in our pain we may sometimes ask, "Why?" we can trust that God's plan for us is good. We will also not resist His work in our life, knowing that He closes and opens doors for our good and realizing that He uses the fires of life to purify our faith and shape us into Christ's image.

Yielding to God's will also means being flexible. As we try to be attentive to God's presence and mindful that

He choreographs our days, we will hold loosely the plans we've made. Although we've asked His blessing on the schedule of the day and the goals of our life, we know that His own schedule and His own plan may supersede our ideas. When that happens—when God reveals His will to us and changes our plans—we recognize His hand and adjust accordingly. Knowing God and expecting Him to make His presence known in our day-to-day life, we bend when He reveals His will for us and we yield to His wise and loving plan.

Sometimes when God acts, however, we may not happily yield to His will. Those times call for us to be submissive, a word whose popularity has declined in the last few decades. Even when we know God and are working to know Him better, we will find ourselves in situations and looking at circumstances in the world around us which we don't understand. Then we must acknowledge that God's ways are not our ways and that He is far superior to us in both wisdom and knowledge (Isaiah 55:8). We submit to our God, again trusting Him because we know Him and His love for us.

Yielding, flexing, and submitting to God's will for us are steps toward surrendering to Him and accepting all that He asks or demands of us. When we surrender ourselves to God, we respect His authority, welcome His guidance and involvement in our life, willingly obey Him, and, keeping in mind the truth of Romans 11:33, acknowledge that He is a wise and loving God whenever we face the mysteries of life and the unexplainable tragedies of this world.

Trusting God's Wisdom

"Oh, the depth of the riches of the wisdom of God!" exults the apostle Paul. He has just written eleven chapters about God's righteousness and mercy, the "mystery" of salvation as revealed in Jesus Christ (Romans

11:25), and the glorious theme of justification by faith. Looking back over all that he has reviewed, gazing at all that God has revealed to him, and yet realizing how much he does not begin to really understand, Paul is overwhelmed by his great God. In this single verse of Scripture, Paul praises God for His wisdom, His knowledge, His judgments, and His ways. In this chapter we'll consider God's wisdom and knowledge, and we'll begin with His wisdom.

When I need wisdom, I go primarily to the Bible. I try to read from Proverbs each day, and I often follow along in a commentary. Also, reading the words of believers who have gone before me and studying the lives of Old and New Testament figures also teaches me wisdom. My Christian mentors and teachers through the years have been great sources of wisdom, and I have never hesitated to follow the example of Queen Esther. She never made a significant decision without first asking for counsel. When, like Esther, I have asked for advice from my husband, pastor, peers, friends, and teachers, I have been blessed and guided by God's wisdom.

God, however, doesn't have to study the Bible or read a book. Neither does He need to seek counsel or advice from others. He Himself *is* wisdom, and A. W. Tozer defines that wisdom as "the ability to devise perfect ends and to achieve those ends by the most perfect means."[2] The writers of the Bible describe God's wisdom as unsearchable, inscrutable, inexhaustible, and unfathomable.

In fact, as I studied various commentaries on Romans 11:33, I found myself needing to follow Queen Esther's example and ask a question about a recurring comment on the original Greek. My husband, Jim, explained that, in today's vernacular, Paul's words would read something like this: "Can you trace God's wisdom? NOT! Can you find it? NOT! Does it have footprints to follow? NOT! Are there tracks? NOT! Can you go to the depths of it? NOT! Can it be exhausted? NOT! Is there an end to it? NOT!" God's wisdom is self-sufficient and perfect because God Himself is self-sufficient and perfect.

And this perfect wisdom calls us to faith. A. W. Tozer writes, "The testimony of faith is that, no matter how things look in this fallen world, all God's acts are wrought in perfect wisdom."[3] Although God's ways are often mysterious, by faith we believe in the infinite and holy wisdom behind them. We exercise our will and, in faith, trust in the wisdom of God that stands behind the events we don't understand. As A. W. Tozer says, we "trust Him in the dark."[4] And as Oswald Chambers so rightly points out, "Trustfulness is based on confidence in God whose ways I do not understand; if I did, there would be no need for trust."[5] You and I can trust our God because we know that He is thoroughly good and perfectly wise.

Heeding God's Wisdom

Having put our faith and trust in God, we are to obey our wise and loving heavenly Father. Soon after I became a Christian, I had an opportunity to choose between the world's wisdom and God's, and I chose to put God's wisdom to the test. My psychology courses had taught me to never spank my children, and I never had. But in my daily reading of Proverbs, I was hearing God's instruction to discipline my two preschool daughters, and I realized that such discipline might involve the punishment of a spanking from time to time. The world was telling me one thing and God's Word was telling me the opposite. Knowing what God said, I knew I had to obey. I even bought a little wooden spoon in preparation.

One day when my young daughters needed to be disciplined, I picked up the little spoon, explained why I needed to do what I was about to do, and spanked them.

This seemingly tiny step was major for me because I was obeying what I understood God to be telling me through His Word. I was, by faith, applying God's wisdom to my life. I had to trust in God's wisdom, allow it to override other things I had been told, and then obey the commands. Without completely understanding how to apply His wise directive to discipline my children, I believed, I trusted, and I obeyed as best I could.

And a miracle occurred in our home. Oh, yes, my children cried—and I cried with them—on those rare occasions when I had to use that wooden spoon. But suddenly my girls started following my instructions and listening when I spoke. We began to have a home of peace instead of chaos. As I offered behavioral guidelines and discipline (and that meant an occasional spanking) for my girls, Jim and I learned the wisdom of obeying the wisdom of God.

I also tested God's wisdom in my marriage. I knew what the psychology and popular self-help books taught about a husband-wife relationship. I had learned that I was to be my own person and pursue my own desires and if my husband's goals and mine were in conflict, the most important thing was my happiness, even if that meant divorce. But now I was learning what the Bible taught, and the idea of submitting to my husband was inconceivable. This was the polar opposite of every voice I'd heard in my 28 years.

But one Sunday morning I tried submitting to my husband by honoring a decision he made. Granted, the matter was relatively insignificant, but it became hugely significant for me as I tested God's wisdom. The situation involved getting doughnuts on the way to church. Jim would regularly and enthusiastically suggest, "Hey, let's stop for doughnuts on the way to church!" Without fail, I would respond with various arguments against getting doughnuts—it's not in the budget, the girls don't need the sugar, none of us needs the fat, and it's an inconvenience to stop by the store. Once I started my spiel, the atmosphere in our home became tense. Our children would listen quietly and wonder whether Dad or Mom would win, a sure sign of who was running the family. The morning was spoiled—all over four doughnuts!

This particular morning, however, I said nothing, and another miracle happened. Our home was joyous that morning. So was the ride in the car to the doughnut shop and on to church. I had kept my mouth shut and given my family some simple fun and a pleasant memory. Also, Katherine and Courtney learned that Jim actually and rightly was in charge. Again, I didn't understand completely why I needed to submit or what difference it would make. But I put my faith in God's Word, trusted His wisdom, and followed through in obedience. And, once again, even over the little matter of doughnuts on the way to church, confusion in my home turned to calm as God's order and authority were established in our marriage.

Like me, you undoubtedly also wonder why certain things are the way they are. You probably struggle to understand why something in your life has happened or not happened. In other words, like me, you may have to make a conscious effort to accept God's wisdom and live accordingly. My friend Donelle learned much about God and His wisdom when she carried a baby full-term knowing for most of the pregnancy that the child would live only a few brief hours due to a genetic defect. But I have a five-page letter Donelle wrote listing all the lessons God taught her as those months crawled by. She learned to accept God's wisdom in His choice of this purpose for her. She learned to trust God in the dark.

Whatever the situation—everything from spanking a child to having your baby die in your arms—we must acknowledge, as Paul does, "Oh, the depth of the riches of the wisdom of God!" When we don't understand and don't agree with the way life has gone, we are to bow before God and once again confess that we can't understand His wisdom. In faith, we are to accept His wisdom, His Word, and His workings, trusting in Him and obeying His commands.

The Knowledge of God

Closely related to honoring God's wisdom is appreciating His knowledge. Even in our fallen world, knowledge is pursued, rewarded, and prized. We read books, take classes, watch educational television, earn degrees, obtain licenses, and enroll in continuing educational courses. We investigate the various branches of mathematics, physics, chemistry, biology, and the other sciences. We plumb the mysteries of DNA and genetics and reach beyond the atmosphere to the moon and distant planets. And we use computers to manage the increasing amount of knowledge available to us in this era of the information explosion.

God, however, doesn't need computers, encyclopedias, teachers, or classes. He Himself is the source of all knowledge and, like His wisdom, His knowledge is unsearchable, inscrutable, unfathomable, inexhaustible, and unexplainable. We cannot begin to define God's knowledge. We know, simply and profoundly, that nothing is hidden from Him or incomprehensible to Him. As the Author of all things, God knows all that can be known.

And among all that God knows is your particular situation and mine. God knows our joys and sorrows. He knows our strengths and weaknesses, and He knows our husband's strengths and weaknesses. God knows our children, their temperaments, their needs, and the challenges we face raising them. And if there are no children, God knows His purpose in that and He knows your suffering. And if you don't have a husband, God knows your pain and how He plans to use your life for Him. God knows our finances and our job, our neighbors and our in-laws, our service to Him and our questions for Him.

And, of course, God knows our problems. The difficulties we face are no secret to Him. In fact, He has known about them forever. The challenges we face are no secret to Him. In fact, He knows—and has known since the beginning of time—exactly how He would use them to draw you closer to Him and make you more like Christ. God's knowledge extends throughout time and includes our past, our present, and our future. Knowing that God knows all these things I've listed makes it easier for me to accept whatever comes my way. The fact of God's knowledge also helps me feel His presence with me especially when life is difficult.

Put simply, God knows all about you and all about me. He knows our hurts, our wants, and our needs, and therefore He understands us. And when a friend of mine asked several groups of women, "What is it that you want?" she learned that we want to be understood by at least one person. Because of God's knowledge, you and I are always understood. We can know that He knows all about us and cares deeply about our feelings, our ideas, and our concerns. We can never say to God, "But You don't understand." We can be confident that, when no one else knows, He knows.

We are thoroughly known by God and, at the same time, we are loved thoroughly and unconditionally by Him. Such love enables us to accept what comes our way in life, knowing that He will work even the worst for His purposes and our good. We can therefore avoid feeling bitter. If no one cared, no one could help, no one would listen, and no one was there for us to turn to, we could be bitter. But because God knows everything about us, cares about us, helps us, and listens to us whenever we turn to Him, we are not carrying our burdens alone. We therefore have no reason to be bitter.

Furthermore, because God knows everything about us, we have every reason to accept His will for our life. He always knows what is happening to us, why it is happening, and what His purposes are in it. When and how the most painful of situations is going to be resolved and redeemed is no mystery to God. Knowing this truth about God's complete knowledge really does help me accept the unacceptable in my life.

Now, for a moment, think back on Sarah Coleman's statement: "Women today have so many problems simply because they don't know God." We've been getting to know God better in this chapter by considering His wisdom and His knowledge. Now, at the end of this chapter, how do your problems look laid before the infinite wisdom and knowledge of your loving God? How big are your problems next to God?

"Oh, the depth of the riches both of the wisdom and knowledge of God!" writes Paul, and the wisdom and knowledge of our heavenly Father help us to accept His will in our life. In fact, I think of God's wisdom and His knowledge as the bookends for my life, holding up all of its incomprehensible episodes and offering a sense of order to God's mysterious working. After all, nothing is ever unknown, nothing is ever overlooked, and nothing is ever a surprise to God. And, as A. W. Tozer reminds us, in all that ever happens to you and me, God in His wisdom is always working toward predestined goals with His flawless precision.[6] By His grace, we can better accept every event of our life when we realize that all of our life is in the hands of our infinitely wise God who knows us and loves us as no one else does.

13

Accepting the Unacceptable

———— ❧ ————

Oh, the depth of the riches
both of the wisdom and knowledge of God!
How unsearchable are His judgments
and unfathomable His ways!
Romans 11:33

———— ❧ ————

The sun rose that morning just as it had risen every day of her life. As she ran through her list of chores, there was no hint that today her life would be transformed from the mundane to the mysterious. But something happened that day which changed everything—forever.

Seconds after it happened, gone were her hopes of the quiet life she had imagined for herself. Gone were the comfort and safety of a predictable routine. Gone was the peaceful existence she and the family before her had known, the existence which had led her to expect a simple and unremarkable future.

When the angel Gabriel appeared before Mary, the words he spoke to her completely changed her life. Nothing would ever be the same for Mary, for she had been chosen to be the mother of God's Son. She would bring into the world its Savior, Lord, and King. Nothing could ever be the same for Mary.

Perhaps you can point to a day in your life that changed everything for you, a day after which nothing would ever be the same, perhaps a day when dark clouds hid the sun. Such turning points in life can shake us to the core. Such turning points can also send us to God, His Word, and His promises.

Accepting God's Will

Did the pivotal day in your life begin normally? Often our routine is well underway, and nothing out of the ordinary is happening—until the phone rings, the letter arrives, or the appointment unfolds. Whatever the event was for you, it signified a totally changed life. Calling such an event "the turning point," Corrie Ten Boom wrote, "The turning point may be announced by the ring of a telephone or a knock on the door."[1] In her own life, it was a knock on her door by German soldiers. Her life turned from normal to horrendous as she entered a Nazi concentration camp.

What are we to do at such turning points in life? How can we handle such a life-altering incident and the new kind of life that will follow? And what are we to think about the unexplainable and unexpected things that happen to us? How can we accept these mysterious events?

We can learn from Mary some answers to these questions. The gospel of Luke shows us how, at this major turning point in her life, she humbly accepted the news from Gabriel that she would bear God's Son. Notice Mary's initial response—"How can this be, since I am a virgin?" (Luke 1:34). The question—a perfectly natural one—received an answer from the supernatural: "The Holy Spirit will come upon you, and the power of the Most High will overshadow you; and for that reason the holy offspring shall be called the Son of God" (verse 35). The birth would be a miracle. That was all the explanation she got. Hardly understanding what would happen to her, Mary nevertheless consented to God's will for her life. She said simply, "Behold, the bondslave of the Lord; be it done to me according to your word" (verse 38).

When God spoke to Mary through Gabriel and told her that she had been chosen to be the mother of Jesus, her life changed completely. For Mary, God's choice meant being pregnant before she was married and therefore being branded a fornicator (John 8:41). God's choice meant trouble with her husband-to-be, trouble at home, trouble in Nazareth, and trouble among her children. His choice meant a life of tension as she and her baby were hunted down, as she fled from country to country, and as her remarkable Son caused violent reactions in the hearts of the people He met. And, for Mary, God's choice meant a soul pierced with sorrow (Luke 2:35) as she followed her Son on His path of pain to the cross (John 19:25). Yet when the angel appeared, Mary accepted the news with the statement, "Be it done to me according to your word."

The Attitude of a Handmaiden

Why was Mary able to accept Gabriel's startling announcement? Why was she able to accept this radical turning point in her life? The first of two clues is found in Mary's reference to herself as "the bondslave of the Lord" or "the handmaid of the Lord" (KJV). In the New Testament, "handmaid" refers to a female slave or bond-servant "whose will was not [her] own but who rather was committed to another. The slave was obligated to perform [her] master's will without question or delay."[2] A handmaiden would sit silently and watch for hand signals from her mistress (Psalm 123:2). Through these motions rather than any spoken command, the mistress would communicate her wishes. Her handmaiden, having been trained to watch for these signs, would then obey them without question or hesitation.[3]

As this cultural background suggests, it is not insignificant that Mary chose to describe herself as a "handmaid." Clearly, she had cultivated the attitude of a handmaiden and an attentiveness to her Lord. No longer viewing her will as her own and considering herself to have no rights, she was wholly committed to her God. Her one purpose in life was to obey her Master's will. So, that day in Nazareth when God moved His hand and signaled His will, His devoted handmaiden noticed and responded. A model for you and me, Mary accepted God's will for her life. Whatever God wanted, this humble handmaiden was willing to do, even though it meant that everything in her life changed—forever.

Mary saw herself as God's handmaiden and so accepted His will for her life. Furthermore, she knew her Master well enough to trust Him and His love for her, and this knowledge also helped her accept His will. Consider her words of praise in Luke 1:46-55, the song known as the Magnificat. "My soul exalts the Lord," Mary begins (verse 46), and her inspired words contain fifteen quotations from the Old Testament.[4] Clearly, Mary had majored on the majors. She knew God and His mercy, His provision, and His faithfulness to her forebears.

As one author has observed, the number of Scriptures quoted in the "Magnificat" show that "Mary knew God, through the books of Moses, the Psalms and the writings of the prophets. She had a deep reverence for the Lord God in her heart because she knew what He had done in the history of her people."[5] Mary knew God well, and—as we saw in the preceding chapter— knowing God and recognizing His infinite wisdom and knowledge enables us to accept what He has ordained for our life.

The Judgments of God

In Romans 11:33, besides praising God for His wisdom and His knowledge, Paul also praises God for His judgments and His ways. "Oh, the depth of the riches both of the wisdom and knowledge of God!" Paul begins. Then he proclaims, "How unsearchable are His judgments!" Here, Paul praises God's decisions and His decrees as He rules over all creation. God's judgments flow from His holy wisdom and infinite knowledge, and these judgments reveal His plans for the universe, the human race, and each of us individually. Through His judgments, God works out His will in the universe He formed.

As human beings, you and I do well to remember that the events in our lives are the results of God's judgments. We are therefore to accept in faith that the events—those of a very personal nature as well as those greater events which, although somewhat removed, impact us personally—are accomplishing something in His plan for us and for His world. Even when, from our perspective, it seems that something has gone unnoticed by God, we are to acknowledge that He is at work and in control of our universe and our life. We are to accept His decisions, His decrees, and His judgments and accept that He has His reasons, which often we won't understand this side of heaven.

After all, how could we even begin to understand the infinite mind of God? We simply don't have the capacity to fully understand God's judgments. Like His wisdom and knowledge, His judgments are unsearchable and unfathomable. The reasons behind His decisions remain in the realm of God, and you and I must rest knowing that they are His domain, not ours.

Being a parent has helped me understand this situation. We parents, for instance, make the rule "Don't play in the street." Does the child fully understand the reasons behind that decree or judgment? No. Does the child need to understand? No. The child simply needs to accept the parents' rule and obey it. And we who are God's children need to do the same. It isn't necessary for us to understand God's rules, decrees, or judgments, and we aren't expected to always understand them. It is, however, necessary that we accept those judgments and the events in our life which result from them even when we don't understand the reasons behind them. Put simply, our duty is acceptance and obedience. We do not need to understand why things are the way they are.

Young Mary certainly couldn't understand Gabriel's announcement of God's judgment that she would be the mother of the Messiah. She also couldn't understand completely how she would conceive the Child. After all, this plan came from the mind of God. So Mary could either argue and question God's action, or she could accept His judgment in her life. Either way, the outcome would be the same: She would give birth to the Son of God. She had a choice, however, about her attitude and her conduct, and she chose to accept this unsearchable judgment of God even though she didn't understand it. She consented to God's judgment without comprehending the how, the why, or the effects it would have on her life.

Similarly, each day, you and I have opportunities to accept God's judgments without fully understanding them. The newspaper and television news report event after event that are beyond comprehension. The world situation, national politics, the moral state of the nation, the state of the family, trends in government, the decline of moral standards—we can't begin to understand these things. We also struggle to make sense of events in our own life as well as the pointless violence and undeserved suffering in the world around us. We can accept these things as God's judgments, trusting—as we've talked about earlier in this book—that He is at work to redeem the loss, heal the pain, and work everything for His purposes and for the good of those believers who are touched by the tragedies. The only other option we have is to rant and rave, struggle and search, seek revenge, hold grudges, and become bitter toward God and people. The better option—the option that allows us to continue to love God with our mind and to serve Him as He calls us to—is to adopt the attitude of Mary and respond, "Behold, the handmaid of the Lord. Be it done to me according to your word." Accepting without answers is one way to love God with our mind.

And such acceptance saves us a lot of emotional, mental, and physical energy. We experience peace rather than the exhaustion that comes when we argue with God, search for answers, or demand that He act the way we want Him to. With acceptance comes calm. We choose to rest in the fact that the Father possesses infinite and perfect wisdom and knowledge and that these are the basis for His judgments, however inscrutable they may be to us. Like Mary, we are wise to consent without comprehension to the unsearchable judgments of our infinitely good and merciful God.

The Ways of God

"How unsearchable are His judgments," Paul exults, "and unfathomable His ways!" God's ways are the methods by which He carries out those judgments.[6] And we must humbly admit that God's ways—the roads or paths He takes to carry out His judgments and so fulfill His purposes—cannot be described or understood by us. The very fact that they are God's ways points to His independence from human beings and reminds us of the vast difference between Him, the Creator, and us, the created.[7] It is only reasonable that we find God's ways unfathomable. The King James Bible speaks of the mystery of God's ways as "past finding out" (KJV), and the Living Bible says simply, "How impossible it is for us to understand his decisions and his methods!"

Like His judgments, God's ways cannot be understood. The prophet Isaiah revealed this truth centuries ago when, speaking on God's behalf, he wrote, "'For My thoughts are not your thoughts, neither are your ways My ways,' declares the LORD. 'For as the heavens are higher than the earth, so are My ways higher than your ways, and My thoughts than your thoughts'" (Isaiah 55:8-9). Again speaking on behalf of God, the psalmist offered this rebuke: "You thought that I was just like you" (Psalm 50:21). Paul's rhetorical question in Romans 11:34 further underscores the mystery of God's ways: "Who has known the mind of the LORD?" The only answer is "No one." We can find great freedom and peace when we acknowledge that God is infinitely superior to us in His wisdom, knowledge, judgments, and ways and when we accept, without understanding, His work in the world and in our life.

A Lesson from Life

Acknowledging the truth that God's judgments are unsearchable and His ways mysterious is not merely a theological exercise. Acknowledging that God's ways are not our ways and accepting that truth has made a real difference in my life, and it can in yours, too.

Over ten years ago, I experienced one of those situations that had me wondering what God was doing in my life. A woman in authority over me seemed to delight in holding me back from growing in the Lord and in keeping me from stretching my wings as I sought to serve

Him. During the eight long years of this painful relationship, I kept asking, "Can't anyone see what is happening here? Don't You see, God? Just look my way! It's so obvious that she's tripping me up as I try to serve You! How can You let this go on time after time?" Every day for eight years—day after dreary day, year after frustrating year—I spoke daily to God and my husband about this seemingly hopeless and pointless situation. I couldn't stop thinking about this situation, and this preoccupation greatly affected my spiritual life. Whenever I sat down to have my devotions and whenever I attended a worship service, I found myself thinking about it. For eight years I allowed this problem to rob me of my devotional time and my worship time.

Help from Scripture

I'd been living with this situation for eight years when I experienced a turning point. The morning had begun like any other morning. Jim was at work, the girls had been dropped off at school, and I was going through my usual daily routine. When it was time for my morning walk, I grabbed the pack of memory verses I wanted to review and headed out the door.

This particular pack of verses happened to be the first one I had ever memorized. I had been reviewing its 72 verses regularly through the years, but this time when I came to verse #72 I heard Romans 11:33 differently. "Oh, the depth of the riches both of the wisdom and knowledge of God! How unsearchable are His judgments and unfathomable His ways!" I said to myself, and this time—after many years of knowing this verse—there was a breakthrough in my spirit as God used His Word to touch my heart in a new way. The message of Romans 11:33 washed me, it washed over me, and it washed through me. God opened up for me all of the unsearchable wonders of that verse and gave me freedom from my eight-year struggle with this woman.

What happened? Why did that familiar Scripture suddenly come alive to me? All I know is that, as I said the verse to myself, I found myself emphasizing the fact of *God's* wisdom, *God's* knowledge, *His* judgments, and *His* ways. There was no "me" in this verse; there was only God. And the fact that His wisdom, knowledge, judgments, and ways are unsearchable and "past finding out" was made personal to me. I saw that day that this truth spoke directly to my situation.

I remember stopping and saying aloud, "GOD did this! HE allowed this, HE planned this, HE brought this, HE knows this. My situation is a part of HIS wisdom, HIS knowledge, HIS judgments, HIS ways—and those are past finding out!" Freedom came as I realized right there on the sidewalk of a residential street in the San Fernando Valley that I didn't have to know or understand what was going on, that not understanding was okay, and that the situation—which was and always had been in the hands of my loving heavenly Father—would be okay.

God had used Romans 11:33 in other ways before that special morning, but when He spoke to me about the ongoing situation which had been such a burden for so long, I was so glad that I had memorized this verse. God's Holy Word is an instrument He can use in our life to guide, comfort, correct, rebuke, and teach. The passages we commit to memory are like a surgeon's sterilized tools carefully arranged on instrument trays and ready for His expert use. When there is a need in our life, God can pick up exactly the verse we need and cut right to our heart. He did so for me during that morning walk, and the surgery He performed on me with His Word set me free.

Instruments in God's Hands

Each fall when Jim was a student at Talbot Theological Seminary, I would drive for an hour in five o'clock freeway traffic to attend the opening session of the wives' fellowship. At these sessions, Dr. Carol Talbot would tell stunning stories of how God enabled her to serve Him as a missionary, a prisoner of war, and the wife of Louis Talbot.

One fall Mrs. Talbot talked about the impetigo she suffered from severely when she was a missionary in India. She underwent nine surgeries during the 17 years she battled this disease, and that battle was almost enough to cause her to give up her missions effort. But one thing kept her from packing her bags and returning home. Every time she wanted to quit, God would bring to her mind a verse she had memorized. She would dismiss it—only to have another one rush in to take its place. She would dismiss that one, too, but again God would send another one, and another, and another. Because she had memorized too many verses, she said, she was unable to forsake her missionary service. In her final analysis, she shared, "God was using my disease to turn me from a pygmy into a giant."

Memorized Scripture can indeed turn us pygmies in the faith into giants. When we love God with our mind and commit His Word to memory, He uses those pieces of Scripture as instruments for our growth in Him. When we have stored His Word in our mind, God draws from what we know and uses just the truth we need at just the time we need it and in just the way we need. That is what happened to me that morning.

Accepting God's Will

Through the years, God has used the lesson which Romans 11:33 teaches about Him to help me live out each day for Him. The following truths, drawn from this single verse, give me a lens through which to look at everything that happens to me. Consider the peace and freedom which this perspective on our life can offer:

> I don't have to understand everything.
> I can't understand everything.
> I can let go of my need to know.
> I can let God be God.
> These are God's judgments.
> These are God's ways.
> Vengeance is the Lord's.

For eight years, I wasted time and emotional energy on a situation that was causing me real distress—but it was a situation God knew about and had allowed. Eight years were consumed because I did not understand that the situation was evidence of God's unsearchable wisdom and knowledge, evidence of His unfathomable judgments and ways. I still don't understand the reasons why it happened, but now I am free. I can accept that God's ways aren't my ways, and I don't need to understand. Finally, because of all God has taught me through Romans 11:33, I am also determined never to waste my time or emotional energy like that again. Instead, I want to accept that God's judgments and ways are not like mine, defer to His wisdom and knowledge, and say, like Mary, "Behold, the bondslave of the Lord; be it done to me according to your word."

What greater way is there to show our love for God than to fully accept His will and His ways in our life? This ability to accept His hand in our life comes more easily when we seek to love Him with all our mind. It is my prayer that, after studying the six Scriptures we've looked at in this book, you will want to give God's Word a more prominent place in your thinking by memorizing it, meditating on it, and studying it and thereby drawing closer to the God who loves you and allowing Him to release His power in your life as you serve and follow Him.

... Still Changing

————— ❧ —————

"I SURVIVED THE 6.6 NORTHRIDGE EARTH-QUAKE!" Here in the Los Angeles area, sweatshirts bearing that message are currently the rage, but I don't think I'll buy one. I don't need that kind of reminder that I survived. It's a morning I will never forget....

My normal weekday routine begins at four. Knowing that the week of January 17 would be busy, I had faithfully set the alarm for 4 A.M., but this particular day I had indulged in twenty extra minutes of rest. At 4:20, I began my wake-up routine, tempted to sleep even more because Jim was gone. Gathering my glasses, robe, and slippers, I made my way downstairs. Dropping my robe and slippers on a dining room chair, I went into the kitchen to fill my teapot and boil water.

When I turned on the kitchen light, the first thing I saw was a stack of newspapers sitting on the counter, ready for our weekly trash pickup later that morning. For some reason, I decided to put them into our recycling bin in the garage before I filled the tea kettle and got the water boiling. Gathering the papers, I walked back through the dining room toward the entryway and the door to the garage. As I reached for the doorknob, I was thrown into the door. (I still have the dark bruise from the impact of the doorknob against my hip.) I looked up at the entryway light above me, which was swinging wildly before it suddenly went dark. The electricity was out within a split second of the ground's first jolt.

"It's an earthquake!" Plaster fell on my head, and I was overwhelmed by the terrifying roar and rumble of the earth, sounds of splitting boards, collapsing block walls, shattering glass, falling furniture, and the slam of a tidal wave from the backyard pool against the sliding glass door. "This is the BIG one! I have to get out of this house!"

As I tried to make my way the three feet to the front door, I was thrown against the wall six feet away. Reeling but still clutching my newspapers, I tried again to reach the door and this time was thrust five feet against the other entryway wall. Groping, I finally felt the doorknob in my hand. Now all I had to do was find and unlock the dead bolt. But finding it made no difference. The quake was twisting and contorting the doors. I cried, "God, I can't get out!"

Between the thrusts and rolls of the earth, I managed to open the door. I dropped the newspapers and ran, barefoot and in my nightshirt, out of the house. At the end of our driveway, I fought to remain standing for the remaining eight horrific seconds of the magnitude 6.6 quake. Neighbors flooded out of their homes, and we stood in clusters, literally holding each other up as the giant aftershocks began rumbling through, attacking our homes as well as our nerves.

For two-and-a-half hours in the early-morning darkness, we huddled under blankets and waited in our cars. Behind us, the black sky burned with a sick orange hue. We found out later that forty mobile homes two miles across the freeway had burned to the ground. Then we heard—and felt—a new sound. Three booming explosions shook our cars as the gas main on our street ignited. Now the sky in front of us burned with the same awful glow we had seen in the distance.

The radio stations, based in Los Angeles, didn't yet have reporters and helicopters in the northern San Fernando Valley where we were and where, we would learn later, the damage was most extensive. For the time being, we had no way of knowing what was happening.

At last, the sun began to rise. I was shaking from the cold, the unending aftershocks, and the adrenaline racing through my body. I was also dreading going back into our home. I couldn't imagine what the inside must be like. It was then that a verse of Scripture came to mind—"This is the day which the Lord hath made; we will rejoice and be glad in it." But how could I rejoice, Lord? How could I be glad for this, Lord?

Two hours and 29 minutes after the initial quake, Jim drove into the driveway and we entered the house. As we waded through the newspapers I had dropped just outside the front door, God began to use in new ways each of the six Scriptures in this book.

Making a pathway to the kitchen, we saw that part of the ceiling had fallen in and that all of our cupboards were open. The dishwasher and drawers had also flown open. Broken dishes were in the sink and on the floor, the counters, and the stove. I exclaimed, "Jim, what if I had been in the kitchen? I would have been buried, injured, and cut to slivers! What if I had lighted the burner to boil water for my coffee? There could have been a fire, an explosion, and our house could have burned to the ground! What if . . . ?" And Jim—faithful friend, husband, and godly leader, my Jim who has read this book a half-dozen times, heard my tapes, and read the study guide—said, "Liz, it's time to practice what you preach. Remember Philippians 4:8? 'Whatsoever things are true [or real] . . . think on these things.' Liz, what is true? What is real? You weren't in the kitchen." This reminder was to be repeated throughout the next several days as we worked our way through the various rooms of our home.

When we opened the garage door, I sobbed, "What if I had made it into the garage to put the newspapers into the recycling bin? I would have been under all these paint cans and overturned shelves. What if . . . ?" Again,

God used Philippians 4:8 to redirect my thoughts to Him and how He had so graciously protected me.

For three days, Jim and I focused on merely surviving. We shoveled out the kitchen, the entryway, and the family room, dug our cars out of the garage, and began camping out. We had no electricity, no water, no gas, no heat, and no phone. Getting food and water was a problem, and our nerves were on edge as each new aftershock—still coming with staggering intensity—pumped us full of fresh adrenaline.

Finally we worked our way to other rooms of the house. We had to force the door to my office open, and when we did so, we saw that it was the site of the greatest destruction. My office! My sanctuary! When my daughter Katherine saw it, she burst into tears, knowing that I spend up to 18 hours a day in that room. She imagined, "What if . . . ?" I had already beaten her to that thought. "What if I had been in that room? If I had gotten up at four, I would have been sitting on the couch there with my Bible, prayer book, and coffee. And I would have been buried, probably killed by the seven-foot wall unit, loaded with books, bookends, and office equipment, that had shattered as it fell on my couch. What if . . . ?" Again God's Spirit used Philippians 4:8 to remind me to think on what is true or real and so draw closer to Him. I had not been in my office, the garage, or the kitchen. I was safe. I was alive. God had protected me. That is true. That is real.

I did fairly well coping with the aftermath of the quake—until Jim had to go to work three days later. Then I was home alone—alone with my fears and alone as it grew dark outside. All I wanted to do was sit in numb fear, waiting for the next aftershock and watching hour after hour of horrifying but mesmerizing news coverage. But through Matthew 6:34, Christ called me to deal with today and not be anxious about tomorrow . . . or the next aftershock. So I forced myself to make a list of things to do and to start doing them. I focused on the work at hand, not on the fears of the future—fears of another quake, more aftershocks, and what I would do if the earth started moving again. Beyond these fears for my safety, I worried about the financial implications of the damage to our home, how rebuilding would interrupt daily living, and the setbacks that would result in my already too-busy schedule. My list of fears and worries went on and on. But again and again God offered me relief, peace, and hope through Matthew 6:34. He called me to Himself; He called me not to worry.

God has also been telling me, through Philippians 3:13 and 14, to forget what lies behind and reach for what is ahead. The earthquake is over. I need now to address the tasks at hand and press on. I have had to quit looking back.

I have also had to resist the temptation to ask, "Why, God? What is going on? What are You doing?" God has used Romans 8:28 to offer me daily reassurance that He causes all things to work together for good. Yes, the earthquake was destructive and horrible, and the aftermath continues to be horrible, but already I'm seeing God bring some good out of it. We have grown closer to our neighbors as well as our family members. Katherine and Courtney, ages 23 and 24, thought first of us, as we did of them. We wanted to be together, see each other, spend time with one another, and pray together. Jim's mother's home suffered no damage, and she has taken us in, cooked for us, and provided a haven of peace and order. God is working good out of the bad. I am seeing beauty arise from ashes, experiencing joy despite sorrow, and finding reasons to praise despite the heaviness. And I'm sure that for years we will be discovering how God is working good from this rubble.

And so many of us are dealing with rubble right now. Just last night I encouraged our seminary wives—women who come from places across the country and around the world where there are no earthquakes—about the promise of Jeremiah 29:11 and its meaning to me during the eleven days since the earthquake. God has used this passage to call me to focus on Him and His promise of future good. He has awakened in me, His child, fresh confidence for handling the far-from-ideal present.

And, finally, God is using the precious truth of Romans 11:33 to teach me new lessons about yielding to His wisdom, trusting Him in the dark (both literal and figurative), submitting to His judgments, resting in His knowledge of all things, and accepting the mysterious, the unexplainable, the unacceptable. Because earthquakes are in God's domain, I am daily learning more about letting God be God.

Yes, I survived the 6.6 Northridge earthquake! But I have to admit that fear has been a constant companion these past eleven days. Every noise prompts a fresh rush of adrenaline that matches that released at 4:31 A.M. on January 17, adrenaline that triggers that inborn flight-or-fight response and puts me on edge. There have been 3,150 aftershocks—and that's 3,150 doses of exhausting adrenaline. Sleep has come only in small increments, just minutes at a time. A slammed car door, a helicopter overhead, a truck going down the street—these every-day sounds get the adrenaline pumping.

These last eleven days have been quite an experience. I have spent one night sleeping in the car, one night on the floor, and nine nights on the couch, fully clothed with my glasses close by, my shoes on, the door open, and the lights on. For five days I had no makeup and wore the same clothes, and I went six days without a shower. For two days we had no electricity and for ten days no gas, no heat, and no water. For ten days, we carried pool water inside to flush the toilet, and I washed my face and brushed my teeth outside using a pan of water.

But I have also spent those same eleven days plac-
ing my faith and trust in God rather than in my shaky
thoughts and emotions. During these eleven days, I
have found myself loving God with all my mind in new
and greater ways. I have also seen Him use mightily in
my life the six powerful Scriptures presented in this book
to remind me of His great love for me. So I extend to you a
fresh invitation to discover the riches of God's love for
you and of these wonderful promises which He can use
to help you handle whatever comes your way. He certainly is doing that in my life.

Thinking on God's Truth

——— ᓚ ———

Whatsoever things are true [or real] . . .
think on these things.
Philippians 4:8 (KJV)

——— ᓚ ———

My Life

Which of the following ideas or feelings do you regularly entertain?

    __ "I'm not really forgiven."

    __ "I must not be a Christian."

    __ "God doesn't know what's going on."

    __ "God doesn't see what's happening to me."

    __ "God doesn't understand how I feel."

    __ "God wouldn't do that for me."

    __ "God doesn't care about me."

    __ Other feelings or thoughts:

God's Truth

• Read Genesis 16:7-14; 21:17-19 and Exodus 2:24-25; 3:7-9. What truths do these passages teach which contradict the ideas and feelings you marked above?

• Find three or four other passages of Scripture which teach the opposite of the feelings and thoughts you marked above. Write out those truths and let their truth replace the inaccurate ideas you sometimes have about yourself and God.

My Response

• Sometimes God's Word says one thing and we think or feel differently. What does this contradiction suggest to you about how God can transform your thinking?

My Life

Now mark any thoughts you regularly entertain about other people:

    __ "I don't think he/she means what he/she said."
    __ "I wonder what I've done wrong."
    __ "I wonder what he/she thinks about me."
    __ "I wonder what he/she wants from me."
    __ Other ways you second-guess people's motives or messages:

God's Truth

• Read 1 Corinthians 13:4-8a and Matthew 18:15. What truths in these Scriptures could help you with your nagging thoughts about what other people are thinking?

• Find two or three other passages from God's Word that address thoughts about others. Make a note of them.

My Response

• Consider what we've learned from Philippians 4:8 and the guidelines of "true" and "real" it offers. What can you do and what can God do to keep you from torturing yourself with unfounded and therefore probably inaccurate thoughts about what other people are thinking and feeling?

• What will you do the next time you find yourself being suspicious, exaggerating, guessing, or making assumptions about someone's behavior?

• How would your relationships improve if you accepted people's words at face value?

Taking Every Thought Captive to Christ

———— ཞ ————

Whatsoever things are true [or real] . . .
think on these things.
Philippians 4:8 (KJV)

———— ཞ ————

My Life

• Check any fears that you have and put a star next to
  your greatest fear.

__ Natural disaster	__ Money/finances
__ Marriage	__ Children/grandchildren
__ Singleness	__ Widowhood
__ Old age	__ Illness/suffering
__ Death	__ Others:

• What "what if" thought do you think most often?

God's Truth

• Briefly note what the following Scriptures say and how
  these truths apply to your specific fears.

Joshua 1:9

Psalm 23:1,4,6

Psalm 46:1,2

2 Corinthians 12:9a

Philippians 4:13

Philippians 4:19

Hebrews 13:5,6

My Response

• How can thinking on what is true or real—how can focusing on the truths in God's Word—help you deal with your fears?

• What will you do the next time you find yourself thinking, "What if..."?

My Life

• What "if only" thought do you think most often? What general areas of your life do your "if only" thoughts tend to focus on?

• Do you agree with the following statements? Why or why not?

"If only..." is no longer real.

"If only..." breeds remorse.

"If only..." fails to acknowledge God's presence and involvement in your past.

"If only..." impedes forward progress.

God's Truth

• What do the following Scriptures teach about your past?

> Psalm 139:13,15,16
>
> 2 Corinthians 5:17
>
> Ephesians 1:4
>
> Ephesians 2:10
>
> 2 Timothy 1:9

• What does Romans 8:28-29 say about your past? What perspective on your personal history do Paul's words in this passage give you?

My Response

• How can thinking on what is true or real—how can focusing on the truths in God's Word—help you gain victory over your thoughts about your past?

• Consider Paul's words in 2 Corinthians 10:5. How can you take every thought captive to the obedience of Christ? What role can God and His Word play?

• What will you do the next time you find yourself thinking, "If only..."?

Chapter 3 Study Questions
Winning Over Worry

——————— ❧ ———————

Do not be anxious for tomorrow;
for tomorrow will care for itself.
Each day has enough trouble of its own.
Matthew 6:34

——————— ❧ ———————

My Life

• Name the recurring issue or upcoming event in your life that is causing you the most anxiety today.

God's Truth

• In Matthew 6:34, what behavior does Jesus forbid?

• How can the steps of preparing, planning, praying, and proceeding reduce and even eliminate anxiety?

• How would eliminating anxiety affect

—You?

—Those around you?

—Your work?

—Your relationship with God?

My Response

• In Matthew 6:34, what does Christ command you and me to do?

• What reason does Jesus give for His command?

• What do you think causes women to worry about to-morrow? More specifically, why do *you* worry about tomorrow?

• What will you do to stop worrying and start following Christ's command to "never be troubled about tomor-row" (Moffatt)?

• Just for today, follow the four preparation steps. Pre-pare, plan (both long- and short-range), pray, and proceed—and see if your anxiety level is lower than usual.

My Life

• List your responsibilities as a

> Christian woman
>
> Wife
>
> Mother
>
> Daughter
>
> Employer/employee

God's Truth

• Review Mark 1:21-34.

> —List the activities which filled Christ's day.

—How long did His day last?

• Now read Mark 1:35-38.

—After such a busy day, what was Christ's first concern?

—By the time the first people reached Him, what had happened?

—What example does Christ set for you?

My Response

• What difference does a devotional time make in your day?

• Design your ideal devotional time.

The time:

The place:

The material and focus:

The length:

The role of prayer:

• What keeps you from having this ideal devotional time?

• What will you do to remove one of these obstacles today?

Living One Day at a Time

———— 🙢 ————

Do not be anxious for tomorrow;
for tomorrow will care for itself.
Each day has enough trouble of its own.
Matthew 6:34

———— 🙢 ————

My Life

• Check any area below that causes you worry or emotional stress:

     __ Finances   __ Adult children
     __ Teenagers   __ Moving
     __ Job   __ Husband
     __ Children   __ Alcoholic husband
     __ Elderly parents   __ Preschool children
     __ Grandchildren   __ Others:

• What four emotional and physical difficulties does Paul mention in 2 Corinthians 4:8-9?

• Read 2 Corinthians 11:23-28 and then list some of the physical problems Paul experienced.

• What five forms of affliction does Paul list in 2 Corinthians 12:10?

• What physical challenges do you face?

God's Truth

• Look again at Matthew 6:34.

—What is Christ's command and the reason for this command?

—Rewrite the command in our own words and personalize it. Let Jesus speak directly to your current situation.

—How can the command of Matthew 6:34 help you deal with emotional stress and worry? With concern about physical problems?

• What does God promise about your needs in the following verses?

Joshua 1:9

1 Corinthians 10:13

2 Corinthians 12:9

James 1:5

2 Peter 1:3

Others:

My Response

• How can each of the following steps help you deal with emotional stress, worry, and/or physical struggles?

Step 1—Preparing

Step 2—Planning

Step 3—Praying

Step 4—Proceeding

Take a few minutes right now to prepare, plan, and pray—and then, knowing that God is with you, proceed through your day.

• According to God's Word, how are we to treat each anxious thought about the future?

• How can God help you bring your anxious thoughts into obedience to Christ (2 Corinthians 10:5)?

Remembering to Forget

——— ❧ ———

Forgetting what lies behind . . .
Philippians 3:13

——— ❧ ———

My Life

• Read Philippians 3:13,14. The apostle Paul is saying, in effect, "I have not yet arrived at spiritual maturity and Christlikeness. But while I am on the way, I am conducting the journey by . . .":

    a. ____ing

    b. ____ing

    c. ____ing

• The first item on Paul's list is "forgetting those things which are behind" (KJV). What bad things or sins from the days before you were a Christian tend to haunt you?

• What bad things and sins from your life as a Christian haunt you?

God's Truth

• What comfort do you find in the following Scriptures?

    Psalm 103:12

Isaiah 1:18

Romans 8:2

2 Corinthians 5:17

My Response

• What will you do when the bad and sinful things of your past come to mind?

• Spend some time in prayer. Ask God to help you begin to take the three steps of forgetting: find the good, find forgiveness, and forgive others.

My Life

• Why was Paul concerned about forgetting the good things in life as well as the bad?

• What are some wonderful things God allowed you to experience before you became a Christian? After you became a Christian?

• How can good things—honors, achievements, and success—keep you from growing as a Christian?

God's Truth

• What perspective on the good things you listed above does Philippians 3:13,14 give you?

• What does Philippians 4:8a—the charge to think on what is true—say to you about your past glories?

• Read Philippians 3:4-6 and then 7,8. What does Paul's experience teach you?

My Response

• Spend time thanking God for His abundant blessings in your life.

• Now ask Him to help you remember to forget when you are tempted to dwell on past accomplishments. List some of the ideas He has taught you in this chapter.

Going On and On and On

———— ❧ ————

Reaching forward to what lies ahead . . .
Philippians 3:13

———— ❧ ————

My Life

• The apostle Paul knew the human tendency to rest, relax, and remember the past. So, according to Philippians 3:13 and 14, what was the first step he took on his journey toward spiritual maturity and Christlikeness? Why is this step important?

• What does Paul list as the second and third steps he is taking?

• Can you say that your entire life—all of your effort and energy—is focused on God? Why or why not?

• What are some of the things that keep you from reaching forward toward God?

• What changes in your mental attitude would help you pursue God with more passion and focus? List any activities or interests you could eliminate or include to focus more upon the Christian race.

God's Truth

• In describing his efforts for God, Paul uses the image of an athlete running a race. Briefly describe a runner:

Her body

Her focus

Her effort

• Read Philippians 3:12. What do you think Christ's purpose and vision for your life were when He first "laid hold" of you?

• What do you dream Christ's purpose and vision for you might include?

• Meditate on the truth that you were saved for a purpose. What does the truth that God has a specific purpose for you mean to you?

• What does "to live is Christ" (Philippians 1:21) mean to you?

My Response

• Take a few minutes to answer the following four questions:

—Who am I?

—Where did I come from?

—Why am I here?

—Where am I going—and what circumstances are holding me back?

• What steps can you take to reach forward toward spiritual growth? Determine which one you will take this week as you pursue God's purpose for you in Christ.

Keeping On
Keeping On

———— ଛ ————

*I press on toward the goal for the prize
of the upward call of God in Christ Jesus.*
Philippians 3:14

———— ଛ ————

My Life

• Review Philippians 3:13,14 and again list the apostle
Paul's three steps toward spiritual growth.

>   Step 1:

>   Step 2:

>   Step 3:

• Paul has been describing an athlete running to win the
prize in a race. Describe the following about yourself as
you run the race:

>   Your body

>   Your focus

>   Your effort

• Why do you think Christians do not always press for
the prize until the end?

• What is the greatest roadblock to your continuing efforts to press forward?

God's Truth

• What do you find most striking about the following individuals who pressed toward the finish in their journey of faith?

> Abraham (Hebrews 11:8-16,39)
>
> Moses (Numbers 27:12-23; Deuteronomy 31:7-8)
>
> Samuel (1 Samuel 8:1-5; 12:1,23)
>
> David (1 Chronicles 17:1-4; 22:5,8-11)
>
> Paul (Ephesians 6:19-20; Philippians 1:13; Philemon 1,9)
>
> John (Revelation 1:9,19)
>
> Christ (Luke 9:51; John 19:30; Hebrews 12:2)

• What inspiration and encouragement do you find in these examples?

• What do you think it would cost you to press toward the finish in your journey of faith?

My Response

• Paul's "one thing I do" was pressing toward the prize. Could you say that about yourself? Why or why not?

• Consider Hebrews 12:1-4. What do the following phrases mean to you?

"Lay aside every encumbrance, and the sin which so easily entangles us..."

"Run with endurance the race that is set before us..."

"Fixing our eyes on Jesus..."

"Consider Him ... so that you may not grow weary and lose heart..."

• List at least three specific steps you will take to make a greater effort in pressing for the prize—and take one of those today!

Trusting the Lord

——————— ❧ ———————

We know that God causes all things
to work together for good . . .
Romans 8:28

——————— ❧ ———————

My Life

• List the difficulties, losses, hurts, and tragedies of your
life which you would like to see God work for good.

God's Truth

• Write out the promise God makes you in Romans 8:28
regarding the things you listed above.

• What does it mean to "know" something?

• What does "all things" include?

• What does "work together" mean to you?

• What end result does God promise?

My Response

• How could the truth of Romans 8:28 change your perspective on and your attitude toward your difficulties?

• Having read the study on Romans 8:28, what hope do you have when something hurtful or tragic happens in your life?

My Life

• Describe and comment on the following ingredients in your life:

Your background

Your abilities

Your heritage

Your husband (or singleness)

Your children (or childlessness)

Your parents

Your current situation

God's Truth

• According to Romans 8:28, what is God doing with the ingredients you just listed? What is the ultimate end going to be?

• Read Romans 8:29. What is God's purpose in all that He allows?

• What do the following verses say about God's other
work in your life?

> Psalm 57:2
>
> Psalm 138:8a
>
> Philippians 1:6
>
> Philippians 2:13
>
> James 1:2-4

My Response

• If God promises to work all things together for good,
can there be any completely bad things? Why or why
not?

Navigating the Maze of Life

———— ૨૱ ————

We know that God causes all things
to work together for good
to those who love God,
to those who are called
according to His purpose.
Romans 8:28

———— ૨૱ ————

My Life

• Paul teaches that "God causes all things to work together for good. . . ." What is the one thing from your life that you find most difficult to believe God will work for good?

God's Truth

• Read Romans 8:28. For whom does God promise to work all things for good?

    a.

    b.

• Read again Romans 8:29. What is God's main purpose for your life and for all that He allows to touch your life?

• Joseph suffered greatly at the hands of his brothers. When he later faced them, however, he was able to look back over his life and see to what end God had been using the bad. What did Joseph say in Genesis 50:20 about the bad of his past?

My Response

• How does knowing that God has only good in mind for you cause you to view the events of your life?

• What will you do to remember this fact the next time something bad happens to you?

• Consider how God has revealed His will to you.

> Who were some of the people used?

> What unusual circumstances were there, if any?

> What were some things you wanted that God did not permit?

> When and how has God stopped your movement in one direction and turned you another direction?

> Chart your life through the maze of God's will to the present, noting highlights and low times.

> Can you see what God was accomplishing in the hard times?

> Can you see what God was accomplishing *in you* during those hard times?

> What do you see about God's will as you look back on your life? When was He at work unbeknownst to you?

Can you see how the very thing you find most difficult to accept fits into God's apparent plan for your life? Sometimes we don't have that perspective this side of heaven!

• Can you pray the following? "Lord, Your Word says that all things—including _____—work together for good. Therefore, I choose to thank You."

Chapter 10 Study Questions
Enduring Difficult Times

——————— &b. ———————

"For I know the plans that I have for you,"
declares the LORD . . .
Jeremiah: 29:11

——————— &b. ———————

My Life

• What circumstances in your life does God seem to be asking you to live with and endure? What difficulties are you currently enduring?

God's Truth

• The prophet Jeremiah was called by God to speak to the Israelites about their disobedience and the seventy years of captivity in Babylon for their unfaithfulness. According to Jeremiah 29:4, what is the direct cause of their captivity?

• Read verses 5-7. What advice does God give these exiles for how to live in a strange land?

• What words of hope does God speak in verses 10-14?

My Response

• In your own situation, what is God's end or purpose for you?

• What comfort does God's purpose give you as you wait for that expected end?

• Look again at Jeremiah 29:5-7. What goals can you concentrate on while you are in your undesired situation?

• Basing your advice on Jeremiah 29:4-14, what would you tell another woman about how to endure difficult times?

My Life

• As you deal with whatever difficulties you have identified, who are the people closest to you? Consider family members, neighbors, and fellow Christians.

God's Truth

• In Jeremiah 29:5-7, what does God instruct regarding these people?

• God calls His people to serve Him and one another. What guidelines does He give for serving Him in the following roles?

> As a wife (Genesis 2:18; Titus 2:4)
>
> As a mother (Proverbs 1:8; Titus 2:4)
>
> As a member of the body of Christ (John 13:34,35; Galatians 6:10; Ephesians 2:10)
>
> As a witness to Him in the world (Matthew 5:13,14; 1 Peter 3:15)

My Response

• God declares that He has plans for us. What do the following two verses say about what you can do to help your plans match God's plans for your life?

  Psalm 37:4

  Proverbs 16:3

• What specific ways do you or will you delight yourself in the Lord and commit your works to Him?

Becoming God's Masterpiece

——————— ?a ———————

"For I know the plans that I have for you,"
declares the LORD, "plans for welfare
and not for calamity
to give you a future and a hope."
Jeremiah 29:11

——————— ?a ———————

My Life

• When life is difficult, it's easy to doubt God, wonder about His goodness, and question His wisdom. What do you think the Israelites were thinking and feeling as they faced seventy years of exile in a foreign land?

• If you had been one of the Israelites, what would your thoughts have been?

• Again, identify the difficulties you are currently enduring.

• What thoughts do these hard times lead you to think?

God's Truth

• What do these Scriptures teach about God's ways?

Jeremiah 29:11

Romans 8:28

    James 1:13

    1 Peter 5:10

• What do the following verses teach about God's goodness?

    Psalm 23:1,6

    Psalm 34:8-10

    Psalm 84:11-12

    Psalm 107:8-9

    Nahum 1:7

    Romans 12:2

    James 1:17

• What does Isaiah 46:8-11 reveal about God's abilities?

My Response

• You may think or feel otherwise, but, according to Jeremiah 29:11, what are God's plans for you?

• Through this verse, how does God answer any doubts you may have?

• How does God calm your fears and encourage you through Jeremiah 29:11?

• How does Jeremiah 29:11 help you when you feel hopeless or depressed?

• What can you do to remind yourself regularly of God's goodness?

• God is the Creator and Master Artist of your life. Do you think He would plan something ugly for you? Do you think He is capable of making a mess of your life? Ask God to help you see touches of beauty in the midst of your present difficulty. Write God a brief prayer of thanksgiving.

Chapter 12 Study Questions
Majoring on the Minors

———— 🙢 ————

Oh, the depth of the riches
both of the wisdom and knowledge of God!
Romans 11:33

———— 🙢 ————

My Life

• There are many things in life that we cannot understand. Problems, difficulties, pain, and sorrow seem to have no purpose. What events in your life and/or circumstances in the world do you have trouble understanding? What events and circumstances make you wonder why they happened?

God's Truth

• Read Psalm 139. According to the psalmist, what does God know about you?

> verse 1
>
> verse 2
>
> verse 3
>
> verse 4
>
> verse 13 (When?)

verse 15 (When?)

verse 16 (When?)

verse 23

• What does the psalmist say in verse 6 about God's knowledge?

My Response

• Reflect on the truth that God knows all the details of your life. How does the fact of God's knowledge enable you to accept your circumstances?

My Life

• Note any details that concern you about the following aspects of your life and then meditate on the truth that God knows all about these facts of your life:

Your problems	Your situation
Your husband	Your children
Your parents	Your in-laws
Your job	Your finances
Your physical limitations	Your feelings
Your thoughts	Your difficulties
Your needs	

God's Truth

• Look at the first part of Romans 11:33. What two attributes of God are mentioned here and how are they described?

My Response

• Can you ever say to God, "But You don't understand"? Why or why not?

• How does the truth that God understands you change your perspective on life?

• How does the truth that God knows, loves, and understands you enable you to accept the difficult and painful situations of your life?

• Use the following truths to guide your prayer about whatever pain or struggle you currently face. Receive God's peace as you pray.

> God KNOWS every situation in your life.
>
> God knows WHY each situation is in your life.
>
> God knows HOW each situation will end.
>
> God knows WHEN each situation will end.

Accepting the Unacceptable

——————— ❧ ———————

Oh, the depth of the riches
both of the wisdom and knowledge of God!
How unsearchable are His judgments
and unfathomable His ways!
Romans 11:33

——————— ❧ ———————

My Life

• Describe the worst thing that has ever happened to you . . . or any current and seemingly impossible situation you are facing . . . or the day of a turning point that changed your life forever.

God's Truth

• What do the following Scriptures teach about the judgments and ways of God?

> Isaiah 55:8-9

> Psalm 50:21

> Romans 11:33

• As the Living Bible says, the wisdom, knowledge, judgments, and ways of God are "impossible" to know.

Using a dictionary, give simple definitions for the following words:

unsearchable

unfathomable

inexhaustible

inscrutable

impossible

My Response

• How do you handle shocking news or an unfair situation?

• What would those closest to you say about your ability to accept change?

• When the angel Gabriel appeared to Mary and told her she would bear God's Son, she accepted something she did not understand. What keeps you from replying to the events of life which you don't understand with "Behold, the bondslave of the Lord; be it done unto me according to your word"?

• Mary's knowledge of God helped her to submit to His will. What plan for learning more about the Person and character of God could you put into action?

• How does the fact that God's ways are unsearchable and unfathomable help you accept your personal situation?

• Check each attitude that indicates your acceptance of God's ways and His will for your life:

___ I don't have to understand everything.

___ I can't understand everything.

___ Why ask why?

___ I can let go of my need to know.

___ I can let God be God.

___ These are God's judgments.

___ These are God's ways.

___ Vengeance is the Lord's.

• Spend some time in prayer. Ask God to help you let go of those things about your life which you don't understand. . . . Thank Him for all He has taught you in this study of six passages from His Word. . . . Ask Him to continue to teach you to love Him with all your mind.

Notes

Chapter 1—Thinking on God's Truth
1. Carole Mayhall, *From the Heart of a Woman* (Colorado Springs: Navpress, 1977), pp. 27-31.
2. Jim Downing, *Meditation: The Bible Tells You How* (Colorado Springs: NavPress, 1981).
3. Lorne Sanny, *Memorize the Word* (Chicago: The Moody Bible Institute of Chicago, 1980).
4. Charles Caldwell Ryrie, *The Ryrie Study Bible* (Chicago: Moody Press, 1978), p. 30.
5. John C. Pollock, *A Foreign Devil in China: The Story of Dr. L. Nelson Bell, An American Surgeon in China* (Grand Rapids, MI: Zondervan Publishing House, 1971), p. 183.
6. Charles F. Pfeiffer and Everett F. Harrison, eds., *The Wycliffe Bible Commentary* (Chicago: Moody Press, 1973), p. 1330.

Chapter 2—Taking Every Thought Captive
1. Charles F. Pfeiffer and Everett F. Harrison, eds., *The Wycliffe Bible Commentary* (Chicago: Moody Press, 1973), p. 1330.
2. Elisabeth Elliot, *Let Me Be a Woman* (Wheaton, IL: Tyndale House Publishers, Inc., 1977), p. 42.
3. Elisabeth Elliot, *Let Me Be a Woman*, p. 42.
4. Curtis Vaughn, gen. ed., *The New Testament from 26 Translations* (Grand Rapids, MI: Zondervan Publishing House, 1967), p. 829.

Chapter 3—Winning Over Worry
1. Gail MacDonald, *High Call, High Privilege* (Wheaton, IL: Tyndale House Publishers, Inc., 1982), pp. 30-31.
2. Gail MacDonald, *High Call, High Privilege*, p. 32.
3. Gail MacDonald, *High Call, High Privilege*, p. 33.
4. Gail MacDonald, *High Call, High Privilege*, p. 34.
5. Ray and Anne Ortlund, *The Best Half of Life* (Waco, TX: Word, 1987), p. 24.
6. Ray and Anne Ortlund, *The Best Half of Life*, p. 67.
7. Carole Mayhall, *Lord, Teach Me Wisdom* (Colorado Springs: Navpress, 1979), p. 155.

8. H. D. M. Spence and Joseph S. Exell, eds., *The Pulpit Commentary*, Vol. 15 (Grand Rapids: Wm. B. Eerdmans Publishing Company, 1978), p. 239.

9. *Inspiring Quotations, Contemporary and Classical*, compiled by Albert M. Wells, Jr. (Nashville: Thomas Nelson Publishers, 1988), p. 209.

Chapter 4—Living One Day at a Time

1. Elisabeth Elliot, *Twelve Baskets of Crumbs* (Nashville, TN: A Festival Book, printed by Pilar Books for Abingdon, 1976), p. 18.

2. Elisabeth Elliot, *Through Gates of Splendor* (New York: Harper & Brothers Publishers, 1957), p. 196.

3. Elisabeth Elliot, *Through Gates of Splendor*, p. 196.

4. Elisabeth Elliot, *Twelve Baskets of Crumbs*, p. 18.

5. Elisabeth Elliot, *Twelve Baskets of Crumbs*, pp. 21-22.

6. Elisabeth Elliot, *Twelve Baskets of Crumbs*, p. 20.

7. Edith Schaeffer, *The Tapestry* (Waco, TX: Word Books, 1981), p. 613.

8. Edith Schaeffer, *The Tapestry*, p. 615.

9. Edith Schaeffer, *The Tapestry*, pp. 613-14.

10. Edith Schaeffer, *The Tapestry*, p. 616.

11. Edith Schaeffer, *The Tapestry*, p. 614.

12. Edith Schaeffer, *The Tapestry*, p. 616.

13. Edith Schaeffer, *The Tapestry*, p. 615.

14. Edith Schaeffer, *The Tapestry*, p. 616.

15. Edith Schaeffer, *The Tapestry*, pp. 626, 638.

16. Edith Schaeffer, *The Tapestry*, p. 627.

17. Edith Schaeffer, *The Tapestry*, p. 623.

18. Edith Schaeffer, *The Tapestry*, p. 614.

Chapter 5—Remembering to Forget

1. Charles F. Pfeiffer and Everett F. Harrison, eds., *The Wycliffe Bible Commentary* (Chicago: Moody Press, 1973), p. 1328.

2. Robert Jamieson, A. R. Fausset, David Brown, *Commentary on the Whole Bible* (Grand Rapids, MI: Zondervan Publishing House, 1973), p. 1310.

3. John Walvoord, *Philippians, Triumph in Christ*, p. 92.

4. Kenneth S. Wuest, *Wuest's Word Studies from the Greek New Testament*, Vol. 2 (Grand Rapids, MI: Wm. B. Eerdmans Publishing Company, 1973), pp. 97-98.

5. William Hendriksen, *New Testament Commentary*, Exposition of Philippians, p. 173.

6. Kenneth S. Wuest, *Wuest's Word Studies*, Vol. 2, pp. 97-98.

7. F. B. Meyer, *Devotional Commentary on Philippians* (Grand Rapids, MI: Kregel Publications, 1979), pp. 183-84.
8. E. M. Blaiklock, *The Acts of the Apostles, An Historical Commentary* (Grand Rapids, MI: William B. Eerdmans Publishing Company, 1976), p. 79.
9. William Barclay, *The Acts of the Apostles*, rev. ed. (Philadelphia: The Westminster Press, 1976), p. 64.
10. William Barclay, *The Letters to the Corinthians*, rev. ed. (Philadelphia: The Westminster Press, 1975), p. 207.
11. Corrie Ten Boom, *Tramp for the Lord* (Fort Washington, PA: Christian Literature Crusade and Old Tappan, NJ: Fleming H. Revell Company, 1974), p. 55.
12. Norman Grubb, *C. T. Studd* (Grand Rapids, MI: Zondervan Publishing House, 1946), pp. 50-51.
13. Norman Grubb, *C. T. Studd*, pp. 66-69.
14. Charles R. Swindoll, *Growing Strong Through the Seasons of Life* (Portland, OR: Multnomah Press, 1983), pp. 315-16.
15. H. D. M. Spence and Joseph S. Exell, eds., *The Pulpit Commentary*, Vol. 20, pp. 131, 138.
16. William Barclay, *The Letters to the Philippians, Colossians, and Thessalonians*, rev. ed. (Philadelphia: The Westminster Press, 1975), p. 66.
17. Helen Roseveare, *He Gave Us a Valley* (Downers Grove, IL: InterVarsity Press, 1976).
18. Elisabeth Elliot, *Through Gates of Splendor* (New York: Harper & Brothers Publishers, 1957).
19. Corrie Ten Boom, *Tramp for the Lord*.

Chapter 6—Going On and On and On

1. Max Anders and Kenneth Boa, revised edition printed under the title *Scripture Talks with God* (Nashville: Thomas Nelson Publishers, 1990), p. 139.
2. William Barclay, *The Letters to the Philippians, Colossians, and Thessalonians*, rev. ed. (Philadelphia: The Westminster Press, 1975), p. 66.
3. Oswald Chambers, *Christian Discipline*, Vol. 2 (Fort Washington, PA: Christian Literature Crusade, 1936), p. 149.

Chapter 7—Keeping On Keeping On

1. H. D. M. Spence and Joseph S. Exell, eds., *The Pulpit Commentary*, Vol. 20 (Grand Rapids, MI: Wm. B. Eerdmans Publishing Company, 1978), p. 152.
2. Oswald Chambers, *My Utmost for His Highest* (Westwood, NJ: Barbour Books, 1963).

3. Ralph P. Martin, *Tyndale New Testament Commentaries, The Epistle of Paul to the Philippians* (Grand Rapids, MI: William B. Eerdmans Publishing Company, 1976), p. 154.

4. Ralph P. Martin, *Tyndale New Testament Commentaries, The Epistle of Paul to the Philippians*, p. 152.

5. Ralph P. Martin, *Tyndale New Testament Commentaries, The Epistle of Paul to the Philippians*, p. 152.

6. H. D. M. Spence and Joseph S. Exell, eds., *The Pulpit Commentary*, Vol. 20, p. 125.

7. Carole Mayhall, *Lord of My Rocking Boat* (Colorado Springs: Navpress, 1983), pp. 41-42.

8. Ray and Anne Ortlund, *The Best Half of Life* (Waco, TX: Word Books, 1987), p. 44.

9. H. D. M. Spence and Joseph S. Exell, eds., *The Pulpit Commentary*, Vol. 20, pp. 151-52.

10. Pamela Rosewell, *The Five Silent Years of Corrie Ten Boom* (Grand Rapids, MI: Zondervan Publishing House, 1986).

11. Shirley Price, *God's Plan for the Wife and Mother* (22422 Kathryn Ave., Torrance, CA 90505, 1976).

12. William Barclay, *The Letters to the Philippians, Colossians, and Thessalonians*, rev. ed. (Philadelphia: The Westminster Press, 1975), p. 64.

13. Cathy Guisewite, *Cathy* comic strip (*L.A. Times*, 1992).

Chapter 8—Trusting the Lord

1. Don Baker, *Pain's Hidden Purpose* (Portland, OR: Multnomah Press, 1983), p. 69.

2. H. D. M. Spence and Joseph S. Exell, eds., *The Pulpit Commentary*, Vol. 18 (Grand Rapids, MI: Wm. B. Eerdmans Publishing Company, 1977), p. 212.

3. Robert Jamieson, A. R. Fausset, and David Brown, *Commentary on the Whole Bible* (Grand Rapids, MI: Zondervan Publishing House, 1973), p. 1163.

4. William Hendriksen, *New Testament Commentary, Exposition of Philippians* (Grand Rapids: MI: Baker Book House, 1975), p. 280.

5. John F. MacArthur, *The MacArthur New Testament Commentary, Romans 1-8* (Chicago: Moody Press, 1991), p. 473.

6. John F. MacArthur, *The MacArthur New Testament Commentary, Romans 1-8*, p. 473.

7. Dwight L. Moody, *Notes from My Bible and Thoughts from My Library* (Grand Rapids: Baker Book House, 1979), p. 256.

8. Kenneth S. Wuest, *Wuest's Word Studies from the Greek New Testament*, Vol. I (Grand Rapids, MI: Wm. B. Eerdmans Publishing Company, 1974), p. 143.

Chapter 9—Navigating the Maze of Life

1. Ney Bailey, *Faith Is Not a Feeling* (San Bernardino, CA: Here's Life Publishers, Inc., 1978), pp. 1, 3, 5.
2. Charles R. Swindoll, *Joseph: From Pit to Pinnacle*, Bible Study Guide (Fullerton, CA: Insight for Living, 1982), p. i.
3. F. F. Bruce, *The Epistle of Paul to the Romans* (Grand Rapids, MI: Wm. B. Eerdmans Publishing Company, 1963), p. 176.
4. Kenneth S. Wuest, *Wuest's Word Studies from the Greek New Testament*, Vol. I (Grand Rapids, MI: Wm. B. Eerdmans Publishing Company, 1974), p. 142.
5. William Hendriksen, *New Testament Commentary, Exposition of Paul's Epistle to the Romans*, Vol. I (Grand Rapids, MI: Baker Book House, 1980), p. 281.
6. Alan Redpath, *Victorious Christian Living* (Old Tappan, NJ: Fleming H. Revell, 1951), p. 166.
7. M. R. DeHaan and Henry G. Bosch, *Bread for Each Day* (Grand Rapids, MI: Zondervan Publishing House, 1962), June 23.

Chapter 10—Enduring Difficult Times

1. H. D. M. Spence and Joseph S. Exell, eds., *The Pulpit Commentary*, Vol. 11 (Grand Rapids, MI: Wm. B. Eerdmans Publishing Company, 1978), p. 596.
2. Irving L. Jensen, *Everyman's Bible Commentary, Jeremiah* (Chicago: Moody Press, 1966), p. 83.
3. John W. Cowart, *People Whose Faith Got Them Into Trouble* (Downers Grove, IL: InterVarsity Press, 1990), pp. 73, 76.
4. Norman Grubb, *C. T. Studd* (Grand Rapids, MI: Zondervan Publishing House, 1946), p. 161.
5. John W. Cowart, *People Whose Faith Got Them Into Trouble*, p. 112.
6. *Life Application Bible* (Wheaton, IL: Tyndale House Publishers, 1988), p. 1089.
7. Curtis Vaughan, *The Old Testament Books of Poetry from 26 Translations* (Grand Rapids, MI: Zondervan Bible Publishers, 1973), p. 220.
8. Julie Nixon Eisenhower, *Special People* (Hillsboro, OR: Thomas Publications, 1990), p. 44.
9. E. M. Blaiklock, *Psalms for Living*, Vol. 1 (Philadelphia and New York: A. J. Holman, a division of J. B. Lippincott Co., 1977), p. 94.
10. E. M. Blaiklock, *Psalms for Living*, Vol. 1, p. 94.

Chapter 11—Becoming God's Masterpiece

1. Edith Schaeffer, *What Is a Family?* (Old Tappan, NJ: Fleming H. Revell Company, 1975), pp. 183-84.

2. H. D. M. Spence and Joseph S. Exell, eds., *The Pulpit Commentary*, Vol. 11, p. 587.
3. H. D. M. Spence and Joseph S. Exell, eds., *The Pulpit Commentary*, Vol. 11, p. 587.
4. Robert Jamieson, A. R. Fausset, and David Brown, *Commentary on the Whole Bible* (Grand Rapids, MI: Zondervan Publishing Company, 1977), p. 631.

Chapter 12—Majoring on the Minors
1. A. W. Tozer, *The Knowledge of the Holy* (New York: Harper & Row Publishers, 1961), p. 10.
2. A. W. Tozer, *The Knowledge of the Holy*, p. 66.
3. A. W. Tozer, *The Knowledge of the Holy*, p. 68.
4. A. W. Tozer, *The Knowledge of the Holy*, p. 69.
5. Oswald Chambers, *He Shall Glorify Me* (Fort Washington, PA: Christian Literature Crusade, 1946), p. 52.
6. A. W. Tozer, *The Knowledge of the Holy*, p. 66.

Chapter 13—Accepting the Unacceptable
1. C. C. Carlson, *Corrie Ten Boom: Her Life, Her Faith* (Old Tappan, NJ: F. H. Revell Co., 1983), p. 83.
2. Harold D. Foos, *James: Faith in Practice* (Chicago: Moody Correspondence School, 1984), p. 29.
3. James M. Freeman, *Manners and Customs of the Bible* (Plainfield, NJ: Logos International, 1972), p. 231.
4. Charles Caldwell Ryrie, *The Ryrie Study Bible* (Chicago: Moody Press, 1978), p. 1544.
5. Gien Karssen, *Her Name Is Woman* (Colorado Springs, CO: NavPress, 1975), p. 131.
6. Robert Jamieson, A. R. Fausset, David Brown, *Commentary on the Whole Bible* (Grand Rapids, MI: Zondervan Publishing House, 1973), p. 1173.
7. Charles F. Pfeiffer and Everett F. Harrison, eds., *The Wycliffe Bible Commentary* (Chicago: Moody Press, 1973), p. 1219.

About the Author

Elizabeth George is a bestselling author and speaker whose passion is to teach the Bible in a way that changes women's lives. For information about Elizabeth's books or speaking ministry, to sign up for her mailings, or to share how God has used this book in your life, please write to Elizabeth at:

Elizabeth George
P.O. Box 2879
Belfair, WA 98528

Toll-free fax/phone: 1-800-542-4611
www.elizabethgeorge.com

Books by Elizabeth George

Beautiful in God's Eyes—The Treasures of the Proverbs 31 Woman
Life Management for Busy Women
Life Management for Busy Women Growth & Study Guide
The Lord Is My Shepherd—12 Promises for Every Woman
Loving God with All Your Mind
A Woman After God's Own Heart®
A Woman After God's Own Heart® Deluxe Edition
A Woman After God's Own Heart® Audiobook
A Woman After God's Own Heart® Growth & Study Guide
A Woman After God's Own Heart® Prayer Journal
A Woman's High Calling—10 Essentials for Godly Living
A Woman's High Calling Growth & Study Guide
A Woman's Walk with God—Growing in the Fruit of the Spirit
A Woman's Walk with God Growth & Study Guide
Women Who Loved God—365 Days with the Women of the Bible

A Woman After God's Own Heart® Bible Study Series
Walking in God's Promises—The Life of Sarah
Cultivating a Life of Character—Judges/Ruth
Becoming a Woman of Beauty & Strength—Esther
Nurturing a Heart of Humility—The Life of Mary
Experiencing God's Peace—Philippians
Pursuing Godliness—1 Timothy
Growing in Wisdom & Faith—James
Putting On a Gentle & Quiet Spirit—1 Peter

Children's Books
God's Wisdom for Little Girls—Virtues & Fun from Proverbs 31
God's Wisdom for Little Boys—Character Building Fun from Proverbs
(Co-authored by Jim George)
God's Little Girl Is Helpful
God's Little Girl Is Kind